Orienteering

Orienteering

Ian Bratt

First published in 2002 by
New Holland Publishers Ltd
London • Cape Town • Sydney • Auckland
www.newhollandpublishers.com

US edition published by Stackpole Books

All inquiries should be addressed to
Stackpole Books
5067 Ritter Road
Mechanicsburg PA 17055

2 4 6 8 10 9 7 5 3 1

First Edition

ISBN 0-8117-2054-3

Publisher: Mariëlle Renssen
Managing Editors: Claudia Dos Santos, Simon Pooley
Managing Art Editor: Richard MacArthur
Editor: Ingrid Corbett
Designer: Sheryl Buckley
Illustrator: David Vickers
Cartographer: Ruedi Siegenthaler
Production: Myrna Collins
Consultants: Ned Paul, Colin Dutkiewicz

Reproduction by Hirt & Carter (Cape) Pty Ltd
Printed and bound in Singapore by Craft Print (Pte) Ltd

Library of Congress Cataloging-in-Publication Data
Bratt, Ian.
Orienteering / Ian Bratt.
p. cm.
Includes index.
ISBN 0-8117-2054-3 (alk. paper)
1. Orienteering--Handbooks, manuals, etc. I. Title.

GV200.4 B73

796.58—dc21   2002022537

Disclaimer

Author's acknowledgments

I would like to thank the team at New Holland Publishing for turning my thoughts into such a wonderful book, and for the opportunity of writing about the sport I have been passionate about for 30 years. During that time I have made many friends in the sport around the world. I would particularly like to thank: Dave Blamphin and Kings School, Macclesfield, who introduced me to the sport; Graham Nilsen or many interesting orienteering discussions; Mike Wilson, Liz and

Pieter Mulder, who have done so much for orienteering in South Africa, for their ongoing friendship; members of MDOC, CUOC, NN and ROC for my orienteering education over the years; all those who contributed to the book, but especially Martin Terry; Peo Bengtsson; Carsten Jørgensen and Jörgen Mårtensson; my parents, Beryl and Geoff, for giving me the best education thus making it all possible; and finally, my wife Val for putting up with an avid orienteer for 28 years.

Contents

Cunning Running

have you ever tried to find your way in an unknown area while driving? One eye on the map and the other on the road? Now imagine navigating on foot, over unfamiliar terrain, often in rugged woods, with only a map and your wits to get you there. Add to this the challenge of competing against the clock and against unseen rivals, and you've just discovered Orienteering!

Orienteering has been called the 'thought sport', 'the family sport' or 'cunning running'. It uniquely combines equal measures of mental skills and physical ability. Part of its attraction is that competitors unable to succeed in a purely physical event such as a cross-country or road race can, by their navigational ability, equal or even surpass competitors physically much fitter than they are. Certainly at a beginner level, the ability to navigate accurately is of paramount importance.

How did it start?

Orienteering began as a series of military exercises in Sweden in the late 1890s and was formalized and popularized through the efforts of Major Ernst Killander of the Swedish army. The sport was initially slow to develop, with competitions being confined mainly to Scandinavia until the 1950s. In the 1960s, orienteering spread to Britain, Canada and Australia, followed by the USA and New Zealand in the early 1970s. South Africa was a late arrival on the orienteering scene with events only starting in 1981.

The International Orienteering Federation (IOF) was founded in 1961 and consisted of 10 member countries. The first World Championships were held the following year in Norway, initially under the title European Championships as no non-European nations were members of the IOF at that time. Today, the IOF has more than 60 member countries around the world and forms of orienteering are practiced in many other countries. The IOF celebrated the centenary of orienteering in 1997–1998.

Taking part

What attracts people to orienteering? Perhaps it is the fact that orienteers get to experience the outdoors. It could be an interest in maps, or using a compass. Many orienteers simply enjoy the challenge of pitting their wits against the course planner and the terrain.

Often, the competition will be in a new area and each event presents a unique challenge. An area with a lot of contour detail will require fine map reading and navigation. A hilly area may require careful route choice to avoid too much climbing. Some areas will be flat and fast. Other areas will be steep and tiring. The best orienteering areas offer different types of terrain, vegetation and runnability (the ease or speed at which a competitor can run over a given terrain).

Navigating around an orienteering course is all about choices. It is about selecting the best route between the controls, and this means the most appropriate route for a particular competitor based on his fitness and navigational ability.

As an orienteer, you are truly tested if you get lost. On a given part of the course you may not be sure exactly where you are, but in extreme cases you may in fact be completely lost. Keeping in touch with the map at all times is critical to success in orienteering, but there is also a skill involved in relocating or getting back on track. The orienteer needs to think his way around the course. Every step, every move should be carefully planned and executed.

opposite AN ORIENTEER MUST NOT ONLY BE PHYSICALLY FIT BUT ALSO MENTALLY PREPARED FOR THE CHALLENGES PRESENTED BY THE TERRAIN.

Family fun

Orienteering is also one of the true family sports. Most events offer courses for people of all ages and abilities and thus members of a family can participate at various levels of competence. There are very few sports where most events cater for all ages and abilities. Courses are graded according to technical and physical content, and where age group courses are offered these are commensurate with the person's physical ability.

No age limit

Many events now offer string courses which are suitable for children as young as seven or eight years of age. The youngest championship category offered is for 10-year-olds, while sometimes courses for competitors of 85 years and over are available.

For family members not yet capable of tackling even the simplest course on their own, the sport also accommodates groups in a non-competitive format. Group orienteering is often used in team building exercises — in this setting teamwork is essential for the successful completion of the course.

ORIENTEERING IS SUITABLE FOR ALL AGE GROUPS.

Let's take a look into the mind of an orienteer:

'The whistle goes. I study the map. A difficult leg to start, about 250m (270 yd). A rough compass bearing and I'm off. Up the hill, over the small ride, past the marsh. The hill gets steeper as I near the top. Over the northeast end of the hill, around the marsh. Vegetation is getting thicker. Out onto a track. Another bearing. Only 50m (55 yd) to the control. Start pacing. Contours are difficult to read. Where are the knolls? Should be easy to spot. Stream to my right. Must have drifted a bit. Yes. Turn left. There they are. There's the control next to the large tree. Into the control, punch and head out to control 2.

About halfway around the course now. Control 10 is next. Head east to the track. Turn left. Follow the track. Glance at the next few legs. 10–11 looks direct. Use contours to navigate. 11–12 is a path run, but I need to choose the correct attack point. Water at the junction, that's refreshing. Bearing due east again. Left of the knoll, straight across the track. Downhill. Bushes on the left and right. Go between them. Now follow contour. Stay above the bushes. Looking for re-entrant. There it is and there's the control.

Nearly there. Body getting very tired. Must be careful not to make mistakes. Head down the slope, very steep, legs protesting. Down, down. I can see the wall and the field beyond. Over a ruined wall, into the semi-open. Avoid the thickets. The control must be at the field corner. There. Punch. Now the run in. Only 100m (110 yd), thank goodness. Finished!'

Scenic splendour

The setting of orienteering events is another factor contributing to the sport's growing popularity. Whether it is a typical Scandinavian forest, a heather-filled Scottish moorland, a wild piece of South African veld, a Swiss Alpine setting or the desolate Australian outback, orienteering events are held in some of the most beautiful areas in the world.

Trends today

Orienteering is now practiced in more countries than ever before. The four International Orienteering Federation (IOF) disciplines (foot, ski, mountain bike and trail) each have their own followings. All are increasing in popularity, with mountain bike and trail orienteering in particular developing very rapidly.

Olympic prospects

Orienteering has been a recognized Olympic sport since 1977. However, the disciplines have yet to make it onto the program of the respective Games. Ski orienteering probably has the best chance as it already meets the requirements in terms of competing nations and there is more flexibility in the Winter Games program. The IOF has applied for ski orienteering to be included in the program of the 2006 Winter Games to be held in Torino, Italy.

It will be much more difficult for traditional (foot) orienteering to get onto the program of the Summer Games. The program is already overstocked and organizers have been trying to keep the number of competitors down to a manageable number.

The techniques described in this book are based on those used in foot orienteering, however most, if not all, are applicable to all forms of orienteering.

THE IOF IS HOPEFUL THAT SKI ORIENTEERING WILL BECOME AN OLYMPIC DISCIPLINE, LIKE CROSS-COUNTRY SKIING.

Getting Equipped

Unlike many sports, the equipment required for orienteering is simple and relatively cheap. You do not need to wear fancy clothes or purchase expensive equipment to practice the sport. Starting out, all you need is general outdoor clothing and a good pair of outdoor shoes or boots. Wear comfortable gear that will protect you from the vegetation and terrain that you will be competing in and, of course, the elements. As you improve, you may wish to acquire specialized clothing and shoes.

Nylon suits

Top orienteers wear special lightweight nylon suits, which allow ease of movement and the passage of moisture through the material. They dry very quickly and are easy to keep clean. In addition they generally offer sufficient protection from trees, bushes and other vegetation through which the orienteer will run.

The tops can either have long or short sleeves as there is generally no restriction on whether an orienteer must cover his or her arms or not. This is a personal preference and the choice may be governed by the weather conditions.

The trousers, however, are usually full length as many countries insist that orienteers have full leg cover. This arose following an outbreak of hepatitis amongst orienteers years ago — it was discovered that the cause lay in the transmission of blood from one competitor to another via cuts sustained on their legs during competition.

The wearing of long trousers is advisable as even the most benign-looking vegetation can easily cause scratches and cuts on the lower limbs.

opposite ORIENTEERS INVOLVED IN MOUNTAIN MARATHONS WILL WEAR LONG SLEEVES AND TROUSERS FOR PROTECTION FROM THE ELEMENTS.

Many orienteers wear orienteering suits in the colors of their club so that they are readily recognizable to fellow club members. At one time the wearing of red clothing in the terrain was banned as it was felt that it confused competitors who thought that they were seeing a control. However, this restriction has been lifted and these days orienteering suits of every imaginable color can be seen at the large events.

Gaiters

To protect the legs further, many orienteers wear gaiters. These are readily available from specialist orienteering shops and are a good investment for the regular orienteer. Usually made of nylon, they consist of a thickened pad of material at the front. The gaiters fasten round the lower leg and will prevent the thicker vegetation from penetrating the thin nylon trousers in this area. This is especially true if the undergrowth consists of plant species such as brambles, bracken or nettles.

An alternative to gaiters are 'bramble bashers'. Essentially a pair of long socks with reinforced front sections, bramble bashers are made with flexible plastic material and offer the same protection as gaiters but with more comfort.

Footwear

Probably the most expensive piece of orienteering equipment is the shoes, especially if you purchase top-of-the-range specialist orienteering shoes. Beginners can wear any outdoor shoes or boots. However, they will soon realize that 'ordinary' footwear is not the best for competition. Hiking boots will survive the rigors of the competition but will prove to be too heavy. Running or training shoes may initially appear ideal but are unlikely to survive for long the hammering and soaking they will get. Orienteering

Gearing up

A SHORT-SLEEVED TOPS ARE MADE OF LIGHTWEIGHT BREATHABLE NYLON.

B-C UNDER COOL CONDITIONS, LONG-SLEEVED TOPS MADE OF SIMILAR FABRIC MAY ALSO BE WORN.

D FULL-LENGTH TROUSERS ARE COMPULSORY IN MANY COUNTRIES AS THEY OFFER PROTECTION FROM NASTY CUTS.

E GAITERS, WORN OVER THE SHIN, OFFER ADDITIONAL PROTECTION FROM VEGETATION.

F ORIENTEERING SHOES MADE OF TOUGH, FLEXIBLE MATERIAL ARE EQUIPPED WITH STUDS FOR BETTER GRIP.

G SAFETY-TYPE GLASSES ARE OPTIONAL – THEY CAN OFFER PROTECTION FROM BRANCHES.

shoes have been designed especially to meet the demands of the sport and the punishment that they will get by being subjected to rocks, marshes, undergrowth and other harsh terrain.

A typical orienteering shoe has rubber studs (with or without short metal spikes) and is composed of tough, lightweight material. It has very little internal padding but is very flexible. There are generally few restrictions on what type of shoes may be worn at an orienteering event but the use of metal studded shoes is prohibited in some countries.

If you intend to get serious about the sport, a good pair of orienteering shoes is essential. There are several companies that manufacture specialist shoes, but while these are readily available in the major orienteering countries, they may well have to be imported into the smaller ones.

Other bits & pieces

When a **control card** is used in competition, one of the best ways to carry it is around the wrist. It can be attached with a piece of string or elastic but special clips are available which do the job much more efficiently.

The protection of the control card is the competitor's responsibility. This can be done either by putting the card into a special plastic bag or by covering the card with **transparent self-adhesive plastic**. Cards that are illegible due to the rain can lead to disqualification. The increased use of waterproof 'tyvek' control cards, and more recently electronic punching systems, has reduced these instances.

A **map case** (1) is essential to protect the map from the elements. The control description sheet also needs to be protected as this is usually printed on non-waterproof paper. This can be placed inside the map case or sealed with the control card. However, special holders are available that can be worn on the arm, making the checking of the control code and description very easy.

Some orienteers like to wear hats or **sweatbands** to protect their head and/or to prevent sweat running into their eyes. You may also choose to wear clear **safety-type glasses** to protect your eyes while running though the forest.

The carrying of a **whistle**, although not usually mandatory, is also advisable, especially for younger competitors and for competitions held at night.

For night orienteering a good torch or **headlamp** (2) is required. Special lightweight headlamps with powerful halogen beams are used by top orienteers, leaving both hands free to hold the map and compass.

For smaller events you will need a **red pen** (3) for marking the course down onto your map, and **safety pins** are always useful, especially if you attach the control card to your clothing.

Useful extras

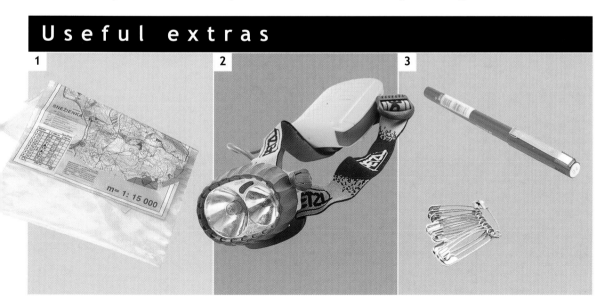

1

2

3

Safety and first aid

Despite the nature of the sport, orienteering produces very few serious injuries. However, safety is of paramount importance at all orienteering events.

Missing in action

The first concern is to account for everybody at the end of an event. It is essential that the organizer knows that everybody has returned safely. This is done by having a two-part control card.

The stub — with the competitor's name, start time and course on it — is handed in at the start of the event. When a competitor finishes, she hands in her control card as proof that she has completed the course. The card is matched to the corresponding stub to confirm that the competitor has left the area safely.

As the event comes to an end, the number of unmatched stubs will decrease until, hopefully, there are none left. If there are, the organizer knows that a search must be mounted for the missing persons.

Report to the finish!

Regardless of whether or not you have completed the course, it is imperative that you report to the finish. You must also report if you lose your control card so that the stub can be accounted for. On occasion, orienteers who have not had a good run or have not completed the course have simply gone home. This has led to unnecessary searches for people who were not really missing.

These days, electronic punching is used in many large events. In this case, activation of the electronic punch card indicates that the competitor has gone out into the area. When a competitor finishes, this is also recorded and it is a simple matter to obtain a list from the computer of who is supposedly still out on the course.

Accidents do happen

Despite all precautions, accidents can happen and they usually do so far from the start or finish. If a whistle is carried, the International Alpine Distress Signal can be used to attract the attention of other competitors.

If you come across an injured competitor, you are obliged to render assistance, even if it means giving up your run. Safety must be the first priority. Unless the person can move with some assistance, it is best for one person to stay with the injured person while another goes for assistance. The location of the injured person should be carefully noted so that accurate directions can be given when help is sought.

If the injured person can be assisted to a place where vehicles can obtain access, so much the better. The location of the person will determine what type of assistance will be required — vehicle if on a track or road, stretcher if foot access is relatively easy or, in extreme circumstances and cases of severe injury, a helicopter.

It is particularly essential to keep the injured person warm so that he does not suffer from exposure. Most events will have first aid facilities available at the finish and it is advisable to get treatment as soon as possible, even for the most minor injuries, to prevent potential complications later on.

International Alpine Distress Signal

The international signal that can be used to guide rescuers to your position is:

- Whistle   six blasts
- Torch   six flashes

Each is followed by a minute's pause and then a repetition. Any reply should come as either three blasts or flashes, repeated after a minute.

Eyes

Running through rough terrain can present several threats to your eyes, namely vegetation, mud and insects.

Many orienteers prefer not to wear protective glasses as these can mist up or get splashed with mud or water and impair vision. If you do choose to wear glasses, secure them around your neck with a toggle string so that they are easy to remove when necessary.

Abrasions

Minor abrasions will remove only a thin layer of skin but still cause damage to superficial blood vessels. In the event of a fall, dirt and other foreign substances may be ground into the injured area, contaminating the wound.

Abrasions should be cleaned as soon as possible, and this may entail scrubbing the affected area with a brush. A loose dressing should be applied to keep the wound clean. It is highly recommended that orienteers have current tetanus injections.

Dehydration

It is essential to ensure that a competitor doesn't suffer from dehydration. In hot climates, competitors should drink plenty of liquid prior to starting a race and make use of drinking stations around the course in order to avoid potential problems. If the sun is particularly strong or if the orienteer is competing for a long period of time, the wearing of head protection is advisable.

Sunburn

Sunburn is the general term for inflammation of the skin caused by prolonged exposure to ultraviolet light. Due to the relatively short duration of orienteering events and the fact that these take place mostly in forests, sunburn is not considered a high risk. However, the use of sunscreen is recommended, especially for longer events and those held in open areas.

Stitches

A stitch will manifest itself as a sudden acute pain in your side, caused by the muscles contracting in a spasm due to overexertion. Giving your body time to warm up can prevent the onset of a stitch. However, if you do develop one, deep inhalations with slow, measured exhalations help the muscles relax.

Sprains

Ligament injuries occur when a joint is abruptly stretched beyond its usual range of movement. Most commonly a competitor will sprain or twist an ankle while running over rough ground.

Many orienteers tape their ankles to prevent such problems from occurring. If done correctly, the ankles can be artificially strengthened so that the chance of this type of injury is much reduced.

If you do suffer a sprain during an event, it is important to rest the limb and apply a cold compress to reduce swelling and inflammation. Anti-inflammatory cream may be required and in severe cases you may need to visit a physiotherapist for treatment.

Taping the ankle

A Use non-stretch zinc oxide tape 4cm (1½in) to apply anchors around the ankle and base of foot.

B Tape support strips between the anchors on either side of the ankle.

C Tape over the anchors once more, making sure that the tape does not restrict normal movement.

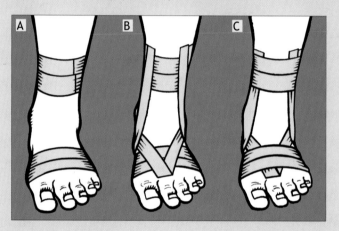

Animal hazards

In some parts of the world large or wild animals may inhabit the competition areas. Their presence should always be respected. A good rule of thumb is to remember that they will generally be more frightened of people than likely to harm them.

Smaller, sometimes dangerous, animal hazards include ticks, spiders and insects. Ticks can transmit a number of diseases including tick bite fever and the more serious Lyme disease. In order to reduce the possibility of catching either of the above, the competitor should check carefully for ticks on the skin as soon as possible after competition.

The use of insect repellent is recommended in areas prone to mosquitoes, and if malaria is known to occur in the area, then malaria medication should be taken well in advance.

Spider bites may look like a harmless mosquito bite but can have much more serious consequences. If you notice a bite on your body and are not feeling well, contact a doctor as soon as possible.

Eco-friendly

Orienteering has positioned itself as an environmentally friendly sport and organizers often display the motto 'take only memories and leave only footprints'. If every competitor abides by this rule, then even the biggest events will leave no trace.

It has been proven that the flora and fauna in an area used for orienteering are not permanently affected; nevertheless, it is becoming more difficult to obtain permission for orienteering events in some countries. Therefore it is incumbent on all orienteers to respect nature as well as manmade structures when competing, to ensure that access to various areas is granted in the future. Any damage to property committed inadvertently during the competition should be reported to the organizers so that repairs can be carried out before further damage can occur.

EVENT PLANNERS TAKE GREAT CARE NOT TO DISTURB THE NATURAL SURROUNDINGS SELECTED FOR A COURSE – YOU SHOULD TOO!

Maps and Navigation

a good map, along with a compass, are the most essential pieces of equipment for an orienteer. A two-dimensional representation of a three-dimensional world, maps have been used for centuries to help mankind navigate around the globe. The earliest cartographic concepts can be traced back to prehistoric rock art, but cartography as we understand it today is believed to have originated in ancient Egypt. The first nagivation maps were drawn by the Romans and later by the pioneering explorers of the Renaissance.

Until Christopher Columbus sailed to the Americas, cartographers were unaware of the earth's curvature, and maps were invariably flawed. It was also very difficult to measure exact distances and directions, leading to very crude charts that were only of use for basic navigation. Today, maps of all types have become highly sophisticated and thanks to modern technology they can be drawn with pinpoint accuracy.

Orienteering maps

There are three important characteristics particular to maps used for orienteering. These are the **scale**, the **contour interval** and the **symbols** used.

The scale

The scale is the ratio of the distance depicted on the map to the actual distance on the ground. Thus a scale of 1:1,000,000 means that 1mm on the map represents 1,000,000mm (i.e. 1000m or 1km) on the ground. The smaller the numerical scale, the more detailed the map can be, e.g. a 1:5000 map is likely to be much more detailed than a 1:250,000 map.

When orienteering first started, maps of 1:50,000 (or 1:64,440 – 1 inch to the mile) were used as these were readily available. However, as the sport developed and maps were drawn specifically for orienteering, the

scales of 1:15,000 and 1:10,000 were adopted as standard. Major events held under the auspices of the IOF are required to use 1:15,000 scale maps unless special permission is obtained to use 1:10,000 scale maps. However, other scales are still used for special types of orienteering events e.g. 1:5000 for park events (*see* p64) and 1:50,000 or 1:40,000 for mountain marathon or endurance events.

Scale	1cm on the map
1:5000	50m on the ground
1:10,000	100m on the ground
1:15,000	150m on the ground
1:20,000	200m on the ground
1:40,000	400m on the ground
1:50,000	500m on the ground

The contour interval

Contours are lines joining points of equal height and form a critical part of any map depicting the physical nature of a given terrain. The contour interval indicates the vertical distance between the contours. On a large-scale map of Europe, for example, the contour interval may be shown as 100m; on standard hiking maps (1:50,000) the interval is usually 25m; and orienteering maps generally use a contour interval of 5m.

The correct interpretation of contours is of vital importance to the orienteer. Not only do contours show the shape of the land, they also play an important part in determining which route an orienteer will select. Losing or gaining height unnecessarily can be time-consuming and a waste of energy.

opposite THE THUMB COMPASS HAS BECOME POPULAR WITH ORIENTEERS AS IT HELPS TO KEEP THE MAP CORRECTLY ORIENTATED AT ALL TIMES.

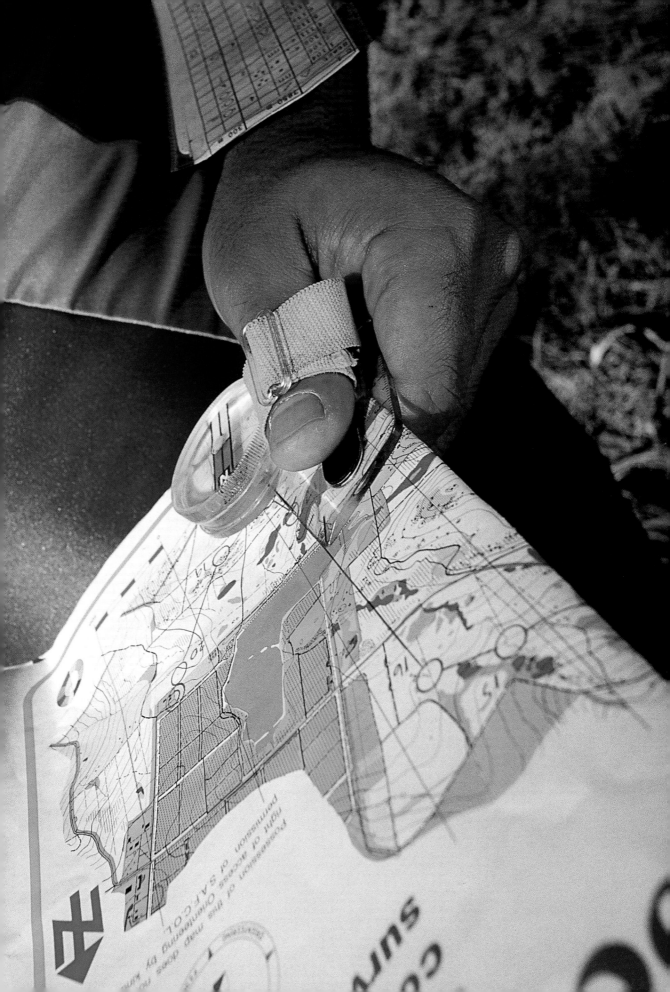

One of the most difficult skills to acquire is the ability to picture the ground from the map. The most important feature in this regard is the contour pattern. Contours on a map depict the shape and steepness of the land and make it possible for the orienteer to visualize the shape of the ground before he or she has even seen it. However, because contour lines don't actually exist on the ground, imagining what the ground should look like from the contours shown on the map is a skill that takes some time to master.

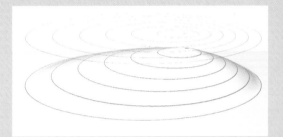

■ Gentle constant slope

Since the vertical height between contours is constant, when contours are depicted relatively far apart from each other it indicates a gentle rise.

■ Steep constant slope

On this slope, the space between the contours is constant, but the contours are closer together. This indicates a slope that is steep but constant.

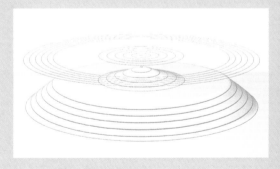

■ Variable slope

Most hillsides will not have a constant slope. Thus the contour spacing will vary with the slope being steepest where the contours are closest together, and more gentle were the contours are further apart.

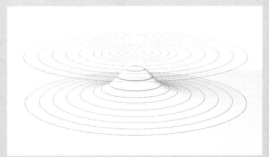

■ Concave slope

When the contours at the bottom of the slope are relatively far apart but come closer together as you near the top of the slope, then the slope is known as a concave slope.

Here are basic diagrams illustrating the variance in contours and the type of slope indicated. Once you have mastered these shapes and are able to recognize various slopes in this basic format, you will find it much easier to identify and interpret the same shapes and inclines on an orienteering course map. A sound understanding of contours is essential for successful orienteering — you can avoid costly errors by being able to visualize the ground through a correct reading of the contours on the course map.

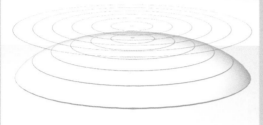

■ Convex slope

Conversely, when the contours at the bottom of the slope are close together but move further apart towards the top of the slope, the slope is known as a convex slope.

■ Terrace

A terrace is a flat shelf on the side of a hill. Thus it will (generally) be indicated by two contours placed relatively far apart, with the contours on either side of these two being much closer together.

■ Hill

Where a closed contour contains no further contours and no additional features, the contour represents a hilltop.

■ Depression

However, if a closed contour has tags on the inside, then the ground inside the contour is lower than the ground outside the contour, representing a depression.

Of course it is easy to interpret the contour detail when shown in isolation as on the previous pages, but the trick is to be able to do it when the contour detail is complex and/or when there are other features on the map to complicate the picture.

Study the major contour features on the section of map below — these may include steep hills and ridges — and form a picture of the terrain in your mind. Be reassured that interpretation of contour detail is one of the most difficult skills an orienteer has to acquire — and it only comes with practice.

The symbols

Symbols on a map represent different features of a given terrain. Thus on a large-scale map, physical features such as rivers, lakes and landforms may be depicted, as well as man-made features such as roads, railways, towns and cities. Orienteering maps, being relatively detailed, use additional symbols which must depict what the competitor will see and enable him to select the best route from one checkpoint to the next. These symbols have been standardized so that orienteers around the world can interpret these specialized maps wherever they might compete.

Early orienteering maps were produced in black and white, because the printing and reproduction was easier and more cost-effective. However, thanks to current printing technology, maps are almost always printed in five colors — black, brown, blue, yellow and green. These colors, along with shaded versions of the same, allow the mapper to depict all the features necessary for accurate representation of the terrain.

Orienteering map symbols are divided into five categories (landforms, water, rock, man-made features, and vegetation), each represented by a different color.

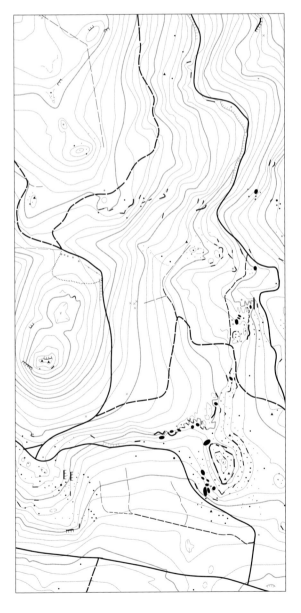

MAP SYMBOLS DEPICT PHYSICAL FEATURES SUCH AS RIVERS AND TREES THUS ENABLING THE ORIENTEER TO PICTURE UNKNOWN TERRAIN.

Orienteering map symbols

Landforms

Marked in brown, these include contours, earth banks, gullies, knolls (small hills) and depressions (holes in the ground). All these symbols help to depict the shape of the land.

The standard contour interval on an orienteering map is 5m (16ft) but where the ground is particularly flat, 2.5m (8ft) intervals are sometimes used to emphasize the physical features of the land.

Normally the 'down' direction of the contour is obvious when looking at the overall contour pattern and the location of streams and valleys. However, when there are no obvious hills or valleys it may be difficult to see which way the hill slopes. In this case a small tag (perpendicular to the contour line) indicates which side of the line is downhill.

Every fifth contour (25m; 80ft), called an index contour, is drawn with a thicker line. This enables the general shape of the terrain to be assessed more easily. When 5m (16ft) contours are used but are not sufficient to show detail, brown dashed lines (see right) known as form lines can be used. These enhance the shape of the land and are essentially intermediate contours.

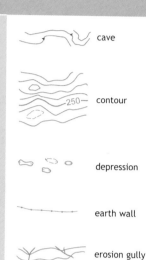

cave

contour

depression

earth wall

erosion gully

impassable cliff

knoll

Water features

Water features are, not surprisingly, marked in blue. These include rivers, streams, lakes, ponds and marshes. The symbols differ if the water feature can be crossed or not, as this will definitely affect an orienteer's route choice. They will also indicate if the feature is seasonal, i.e. if it is there during the wet season but dry during other times of the year. Along with vegetation, the water features in an area may change radically between summer and winter.

marsh

pond

spring/stream

uncrossable river

Man-made features

Man-made features are generally shown in black. These would include roads, tracks, paths (of varying size), buildings, ruins, fences, walls, railways and power lines. Major (tarred) roads are marked in brown. There is a definite relationship between the difficulty of the orienteering terrain and the number of man-made features. If the area has been greatly affected by man's impact and contains numerous tracks, paths and fences, navigation will be relatively easy. The opposite is true of an area that remains in its natural state.

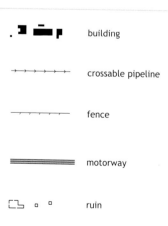

building

crossable pipeline

fence

motorway

ruin

Rock features

Rock features include cliffs (sometimes called crags), boulders, boulder clusters, rocky pits, caves and areas of stony ground. These are also marked in black. In some areas, rock features can dominate and in such cases they can have a significant effect on runnability. Some rock features, e.g. impassable cliffs, can also be dangerous and it is important for the competitor to take special note of these.

	rocky pit
	stony ground
	boulder
	boulder cluster

Vegetation

The vegetation in an area is marked with a combination of yellow and green. However, runnable forest is indicated by white on the map. This is because in Europe the majority of orienteering areas are forested. Yellow is used predominantly for open areas, e.g. fields and clearings. Green is used for areas of trees, bushes, and undergrowth. In both cases, the aim is not to show the type of vegetation but the density, which will affect the runnability of that particular area.

When it comes to green on an orienteering map, the darker the green the thicker the vegetation and therefore the harder it will be to run. The mapper will use a range of green shading from very pale (slow run) to dark (impenetrable/fight). The competitor must judge how much the different vegetation types will slow him down. It is strongly advised that only short sections of impenetrable or 'fight' vegetation be attempted.

Another important point to note is that the runnability is measured, and not the visibility. Therefore it is possible to have areas that are easy to run through but where visibility is limited, e.g. sections with trees or bushes close together, but there is no undergrowth. Where undergrowth is the cause for slowing competitors down, this is indicated on the map using special symbols. Even so-called open areas can be slow to run through. Rough open ground or areas of felled trees can be very difficult to traverse, and these will be marked accordingly.

	cultivated land
	forest: runnable in one direction
	orchard
	rough open land
	undergrowth: difficult to run
	undergrowth: slow running
	vegetation: impassable
	vineyard

Pre-marked maps

When a map is pre-marked, the course (and associated information) is marked in purple. Thus the start, control circles/numbers and finish are marked with this color. Also marked in this way are refreshment points, first aid points, crossing points, taped routes and any map corrections (including out of bounds).

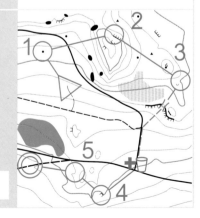

A full list of the symbols used on orienteering maps is shown in Appendix C.

Mapping standards

Although map symbols have been standardized, the drawing up of an orienteering map still requires that the mapper interpret many of the features. What might be slow-run terrain to one mapper may be walk terrain to another; what might be a significant boulder to one mapper may be omitted entirely by another.

It is therefore important to 'get the feel of the map' during the initial part of a course. Make sure that you understand how the mapper has chosen to interpret the terrain and features, and you will be sure to encounter fewer surprises later on.

It is also important to note that the symbols used on an orienteering map do not always depict the exact size of the feature. Thus a black dot of diameter 0.6mm on a 1:10,000 map indicates a large boulder but not necessarily one of 6m (7yd) in diameter. Similarly a dashed line of thickness 0.25mm does not mean that the path is 2.5m (3yd) wide. It merely means that it is a 'large' footpath. However, the relative position of such features and the distance between them is generally correct.

Which way is north?

A very important aspect of using a map is being able to orientate it so that it is correctly aligned with the terrain. At this point the orienteer needs to understand the difference between **true north** and **magnetic north**.

Although the axis on which the earth spins is slightly tilted, the North Pole is still defined as being true north. However, the earth's magnetic field influences the compass needle (which works on magnetism) and slightly distorts the reading of true north depending where on the earth's surface you are situated (*see* p28). The reading taken by the compass is known as magnetic north. The difference between true north and magnetic north is known as the magnetic variation.

Many maps only depict true north (or in some cases grid north, e.g. Ordnance Survey maps in the UK where a grid system is in use for a particular area). In some instances, e.g. street maps, it is not critical to know exactly where magnetic north lies. However,

on outdoor maps used for navigation in conjunction with a compass, the difference between true north and magnetic north is extremely important. Orienteering maps generally only have magnetic north marked on them.

Is the map wrong?

This is a question that you are likely to ask yourself at some time on an orienteering course. Mappers can make mistakes and areas do change with time. The older a map is the more likely it is to be wrong. Vegetation may have grown or been removed, paths may have appeared or disappeared, fences or buildings may have been erected or taken down. However, although there may be minor changes, the area should not have changed so much that it doesn't resemble the map at all. When the ground does not appear to fit the map, the map is likely to be correct — chances are that you are not where you think you are.

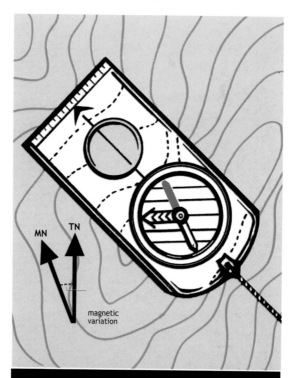

SOME MAPS INDICATE TRUE (OR GRID) NORTH, BUT AS COMPASSES ALWAYS POINT TO MAGNETIC NORTH THE MAGNETIC VARIATION (ANGLE BETWEEN THE TWO) NEEDS TO BE TAKEN INTO CONSIDERATION.

THE FORMAT OF THE COMPASS HAS EVOLVED SUBSTANTIALLY, BUT THE MAGNETIC PROPERTIES OF LODESTONE REMAIN THE SAME.

The compass

There is still some debate about whether it was the Greeks, Arabs or Chinese who first used and introduced the compass, but what has been established is that even early compasses were based on the magnetic properties of magnetite, a magnetic oxide of iron also known as lodestone.

Some 4500 years ago, it was discovered that when lodestone was placed on an object floating in water it always turned in the same direction. This simple concept led to the invention of the compass, which essentially consists of a strip of magnetized steel balanced on a pivot and free to swing in any direction.

The ship compass was developed in the 13th century at a time when naval exploration was rapidly increasing. Hand-held compasses with a liquid-filled capsule were not introduced until the first half of the 20th century. The invention of plastic later in the century saw the development of the compasses we know today.

Compasses are available in many different shapes and sizes, but the most commonly used compass for orienteering is the protractor-type. The Silva company in Sweden pioneered this particular type of compass, but orienteering compasses are now manufactured by a number of companies around the world.

Protractor-type compass

The protractor-type compass consists of a transparent plastic base plate onto which the compass housing is set. The base plate has a large red arrow pointing up the middle, parallel to the longer side. At one edge there are usually measures that are used to check distances on the map.

The compass housing is circular and contains the compass needle. The bottom of the housing is also clear and ruled with red parallel lines, including a red arrow. The compass housing can rotate freely through 360° on the base plate. A cord is attached to one corner of the plate to enable the compass to be hung around the wrist.

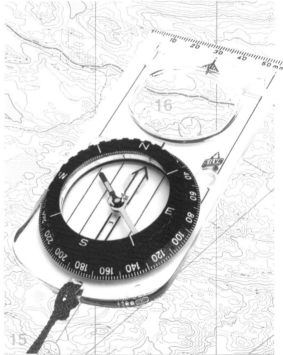

THIS PROTRACTOR-TYPE COMPASS IS MANUFACTURED BY SILVA.

Thumb compass

Many top orienteers have dispensed with the base plate-type compass in favour of the thumb compass. As its name indicates, it attaches to the thumb and is held in the same hand as the map, unlike the protractor-type compass which is usually held in the other hand.

The thumb compass does not have any of the detail included on the protractor-type compass. The main feature is the red north arrow, used for taking rough bearings. This compass is relatively quick and simple to use — the edge of the compass is held along the line of travel and the magnetic north lines are kept aligned with the compass needle, while the straight, transparent edge of the compass can be used to mark the current location, without obscuring map detail.

The advantage of the thumb compass is that the map is set all the time. This is extremely useful for beginners who will find it easier to keep the map correctly orientated. However, it is more difficult to take an accurate bearing with this type of compass.

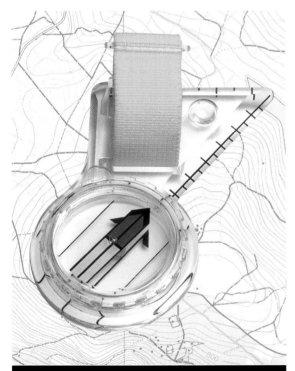

THE MAP IS SET AT ALL TIMES USING THE THUMB COMPASS.

Compasses come in many different models, each with different features. The main difference between a more expensive compass and a cheaper one is the speed at which the needle settles. With less expensive compasses, the needle takes longer to settle and is more easily disturbed from the correct reading, thus giving a false indication to the competitor if not used correctly. To avoid this, the more expensive compasses are filled with liquid to damp the needle and ensure a faster reaction. For top orienteers this is essential, especially if many compass bearings have to be taken during a race.

Other features that will determine the price of the compass are the size of the base plate, whether the compass is luminous or not, whether it has separate detachable scales for different map scales, or if a magnifying glass is included in the base plate.

A basic model will do the job for beginners, provided care is taken. For the more experienced competitor, a more advanced model is recommended.

Is the compass wrong?

Compasses are not infallible and there are a number of reasons why a compass may not show the correct direction. The compass needle may have become demagnetized or the poles may even have been switched. In the first case the needle will not point north but randomly, and in the second the red end will point south.

Metallic objects such as scissors or knives can affect a compass needle and you should always store your compass away from these objects. It is also definitely not a good idea to try to set the compass on the roof of a car or near an iron post, for example, as a true reading will not be obtained.

Overhead power lines can also have an effect on compasses as electricity can set up a local magnetic field which, concentrated in one area, is more powerful than the earth's magnetic field.

If the liquid filling of the compass leaks out or an air bubble forms in the compass housing, the needle will still try to point north but the settling speed may be affected and the bubble may prevent the correct reading from being obtained. It is therefore important to regularly check that your compass is working correctly. This can be done by checking north using a map of a known area. If an incorrect reading is obtained, try moving a few hundred meters and checking again — if the reading is still not correct it would be wise to buy a new compass.

The five magnetic zones

Not all compasses can be used all over the world. Due to the deviations in the earth's magnetic field, the world is essentially divided into five different zones. A compass made for one particular zone will only work correctly in that zone. Thus a compass purchased in the UK will not give a correct reading in Australia.

Today there are compasses available which allow for the differences in magnetic variation and can be used in all parts of the world. However, it is always wise for orienteers travelling from one continent to another to check what zone they will be competing in and whether the compass they normally use will be suitable.

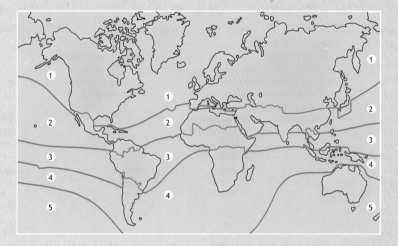

Using the compass

The compass is guaranteed to be your best friend but first you must get to grips with its usage. Top orienteers will easily be able to set the map, take a bearing, run on that bearing and relocate using a back bearing, and it is well worth taking the time to master all of these techniques.

Setting the map

In order to set, or orientate, the map, simply rotate it until the magnetic north lines on the map point in the same direction as the compass needle.

Make absolutely sure that the north arrow on the map (generally depicted at the top of the map, or as a series of parallel lines running across the map) point in the same direction as the red end of the compass needle.

This done, the orientation of the map should be exactly the same as the ground. Look at the features around you to check that they lie relatively in the same direction as those on the map to confirm this.

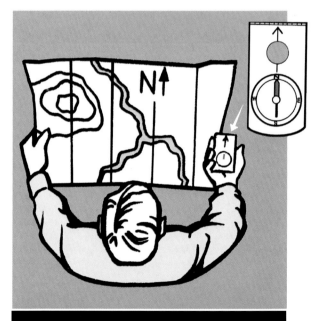

TO CORRECTLY SET THE MAP YOU MUST ENSURE THAT THE MAGNETIC NORTH LINES ON THE MAP POINT IN THE SAME DIRECTION AS THE RED END OF THE COMPASS NEEDLE.

Taking a bearing

When first learning to take a bearing, you will find that you can be much more accurate if you use a compass with a long base plate.

The following three easy steps should set you on the right course every time:

A Position the compass on the map and align the side of the compass base plate along a straight line connecting the point where you are to the point where you want to be. Ensure that the arrow on the base plate is pointing in the direction of travel.

B Rotate the compass housing until the red lines in the housing are parallel to the magnetic north lines on the map. Again, ensure that the red arrow in the housing points in the same direction as north on the map.

C Take the compass off the map and turn the whole compass until the red end of the compass needle aligns with the red arrow on the bottom of the compass housing. The arrow on the base plate indicates the direction of travel.

This method assumes that the north lines on the map indicate magnetic north. If they do not, then the difference in degrees between the north marked on the map and magnetic north need to be subtracted from or added to the bearing as measured by the compass. If magnetic north is to the east of north on the map, the variation must be subtracted. If it lies to the west, the variation must be added.

Staying on a bearing

You can run trying to keep the needle aligned with the housing while following the arrow on the base plate. This is fine for rough bearings but is not as good if an accurate bearing is required.

An accurate bearing should be taken while standing still and focusing on an object, e.g. a specific tree, on that bearing. You can then run at speed to that tree and repeat the process. This is a much more precise way of following a bearing.

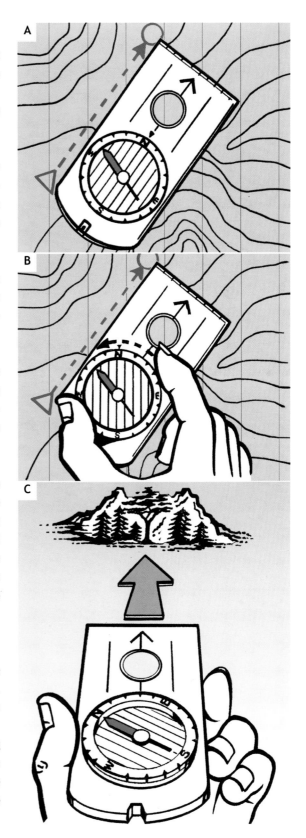

A

B

C

Relocation using back bearings

If you become disoriented and are unable to tell where you are on the map, you can use bearings taken on the ground to find your position again. For this you need to be able to see at least two, preferably three, known points in different directions, several hundred meters away and ideally 60–120° apart.

The arrow on the base plate is pointed at the first known point and the housing rotated until the red end of the compass needle is aligned with the red arrow in the housing. The compass is then placed on the map with the edge on the known point. The whole compass is then rotated until the lines in the housing become parallel to the magnetic north lines on the map, ensuring that the red arrow is pointing north. A line is then drawn along the side of the compass through the first known point.

The process is repeated with the second known point. The intersection of the two lines indicates the present location. There is inevitably some degree of error involved and for a more accurate location, a third known point is used and the process repeated again. Ideally the third line will cross where the other two cross confirming the current location. If a triangle is produced by the lines, the location is somewhere within that triangle.

THE INTERSECTION FROM TWO KNOWN POINTS WILL SHOW YOUR LOCATION.

CHOOSING TWO OR THREE DISTINCT FEATURES ON THE GROUND OR AROUND YOU WILL MAKE THE RELOCATION PROCESS MUCH EASIER.

Route choice

Orienteering is all about navigating around a series of checkpoints using the course map and a compass. The route between the checkpoints is decided solely by the competitor, based on the information available.

The classic type of route choices faced by an orienteer are whether to go around a hill — this may mean running further, but will involve less climbing — or to go over the top — shorter in terms of distance, but will require more climbing.

Similarly, a competitor may have to decide to travel a longer distance through a runnable area or try to cut through an area with thicker vegetation, saving distance but making progress at a reduced speed.

The following are two important factors that should be considered when contemplating a route choice:

The navigational ability of the competitor

It is important that you are able to follow the route that you choose. There is no point in choosing what appears to be a shorter or faster route if you then get lost along the way. Any possible advantage gained from taking the faster route will be lost trying to relocate.

A relative newcomer or poor navigator should opt for the safer but longer route whereas an experienced orienteer with strong navigation skills will choose the shorter but more difficult option.

The physical ability of the competitor

If you are able to run fast along paths or tracks but cannot maintain a reasonable speed over rough terrain or through thicker vegetation, the path option is probably best even if it means adding a fair amount of distance. If, however, you are not a particularly fast runner but can maintain a reasonable speed through difficult terrain, then the more direct route is probably the best option.

To complicate matters though, it is not just a single leg that must be considered. There is no point in using up all your energy getting from one control to another in an excellent time with the rest of the course still to

Making the right choice

Ask yourself these important questions when selecting a route:

- How far are the alternative routes?
- How much climb do they involve?
- Are there any obstacles in the way that will slow you down?
- Can you navigate the routes easily?

come. For this reason it is extremely important to plan ahead and consider the course in its entirety — don't just tackle one leg at a time.

It is clear from these points that no one route is ideal for all competitors. However, it is important to decide on a route and to stick with it. Some orienteers spend so long deciding which route to take that they lose any time advantage they might have gained by choosing a faster route. Others change their minds halfway between controls, a move that can often lead to disaster.

WHILE ROUTE (A) MAY APPEAR SHORTER IN TERMS OF DISTANCE, ROUTE (B) FOLLOWS A DISTINCT PATH AND COULD BE EASIER AND FASTER.

Basic navigation techniques

Thumbing the map

Once the map is orientated correctly, one way of monitoring your progress is to hold the map with the thumb 'pointing' to your location. The map is kept correctly aligned and the thumb is moved as you progress , always indicating your current location.

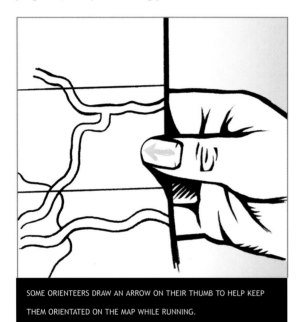

SOME ORIENTEERS DRAW AN ARROW ON THEIR THUMB TO HELP KEEP THEM ORIENTATED ON THE MAP WHILE RUNNING.

Rough bearing

Take a compass bearing for a rough idea of the correct direction. You should be more concerned about avoiding 180° and 90° errors than taking an exact bearing.

Distance judgment

Judging how far you have travelled is a very important skill in orienteering. In order to pinpoint your exact location, you need to know not only in which direction you have travelled, i.e. the bearing, but also how far. Experienced orienteers get a feel for how far they have gone but a more accurate technique is to count paces.

opposite FINE NAVIGATION SHOULD LEAD YOU DIRECTLY TO THE CONTROL.

Counting paces

You will need to know how many paces you take to cover 100m (110yd). This will vary depending on a number of factors, but the two most important are the type of terrain and how tired you are.

You will therefore need to measure your paces over 100m (110yd) under different conditions. This can be determined in an area where you know the distances. Run a known distance and count how many paces you take. Try varying types of terrain and note the difference. Most orienteers use 'double pacing', i.e. they count every time the right foot hits the ground.

If you use pace counting, it will enable you to measure a distance directly in paces rather than having to measure it in meters and then do a conversion.

Rough or fine navigation

There is no point in going slowly and reading every detail on the map if you are a long way from the control. Rough navigation refers to when you set a rough compass bearing and move as quickly as you can towards a catching feature or attack point (*see* Basic navigation techniques, p36–37). There is no need to fine-navigate at this point as you will only waste time.

Using rough compass bearings you can head in the right direction despite ignoring most of the features on the map. If you need to run 300m (330yd) through a block of forest until you reach a track, then all the map detail in the block is essentially irrelevant — reaching the track in itself will tell you how far you have gone. Your focus when using rough navigation should merely be to reach the catching feature or attack point easily.

Fine navigation is used close to the control. It is generally used in the last 100–200m (110–220yd) of the leg and involves taking an accurate compass bearing and/or reading the fine detail on the map. At this point it becomes essential to pay attention to detail and take the time to make sure you are in the correct location. The transition between rough and fine navigation usually takes place at the attack point.

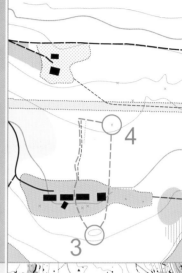

Catching or collecting feature

It is important to consider from which direction you will approach a control (*see* p38). An obvious feature that lies beyond the control is known as a catching or collecting feature. This can take the shape of a road or building, even a fence. If you run past the control, you will come across this feature and realize you need to turn back. However, if you approach the control from a different direction, there may be no catching feature and you run the risk of going a long way past the control, wasting valuable time.

Using a handrail

Wherever possible, inexperienced orienteers should make use of linear features on the map to assist navigation. These features, such as paths, fences, power lines and streams, are known as handrails. If these are going in the same general direction as the orienteer, they can be very useful. Less obvious handrails include ridges and vegetation boundaries.

Contouring

This is the technique of following a contour along the side of a hill, i.e. remaining at the same height. It is easier said than done as often other features interfere or can deflect you from the chosen route.

Contouring is difficult to learn but well worth mastering. It is used by experienced orienteers for two reasons. Firstly, it prevents the orienteer from having to climb unduly. Secondly, the contour can be considered a line feature, albeit one that is not marked on the ground. Being able to follow a contour on the map means that your position is always known.

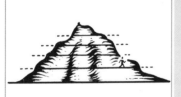

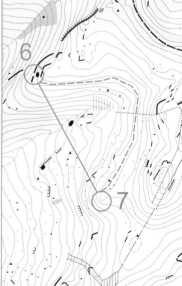

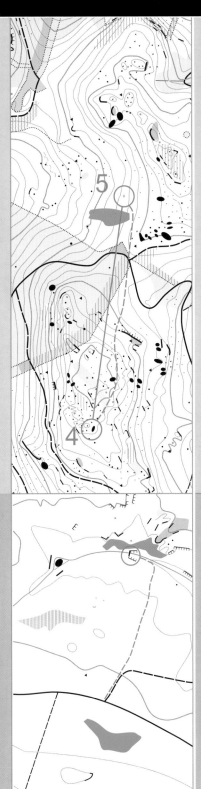

Attack point

Rarely will an orienteer try to locate a small feature by taking a bearing and estimating the distance from a long way off. The errors in bearing and pace counting over several hundred meters can be significant.

It is a good tactic to first find a more obvious feature near the control and then use fine navigation from there. The more obvious feature is known as an attack point. Sometimes, using an attack point may add distance to the route or may mean approaching the control from a different direction. However, the extra effort will usually be worthwhile.

For example, it would be very difficult to find a small point feature, such as a pit, by taking a bearing and estimating its distance from point X some 300m (330yd) away. However, by using a track junction only 100m (110yd) away from the pit as an attack point, the chances of finding the pit are greatly increased.

The availability of a suitable attack point may influence your route choice.

Aiming off

When heading directly towards a linear feature from a distance, it is difficult to say exactly where you will hit that feature. To avoid confusion when you arrive at the feature, it is advisable to 'aim off' to one side deliberately.

If you want to hit the stream at point A in order to find the waterfall, and you aim directly at it, you may end upstream or downstream and not know which way to turn when you get there. However, if you deliberately aim to the right, you know that you will hit the stream below the waterfall and simply have to turn left when you reach the water.

Finding the control

The ultimate aim of your navigation is to find the controls. Sounds simple. So why is it that many orienteers spend ages searching for the control once they are in the vicinity?

Orienteering is not like trying to find a needle in a haystack. The control should not be hidden but placed exactly at the center of the control circle, on the feature as indicated on the control description sheet (*see* Appendix A).

Thus, in determining from the control description sheet the specific control feature you are looking for, you should note its size, if relevant, and where exactly the control is situated on the feature. It is no use looking on the top of a cliff if the control is at the foot.

When approaching the control it is important to constantly refer to the map. This involves fine navigation, taking account of all the features displayed on the map. It will also generally mean slowing down as you approach the area of the control. Sharpen your vision

Control feature vs. control

The control feature is a physical feature marked on the map and the spot on which a control marker or kite is located. The degree of difficulty in finding such a feature determines the technicality of the course.

Line features are easy to find whereas point features are more difficult. However, both are easier than trying to find the control marker directly.

Should the control feature be large, the location of the control marker on the feature should be detailed in the control description. The competitor should therefore be able to find the control feature, check which side or part of the feature the marker is on and thus find the control.

and navigate in to the control feature – don't look directly for the control. Find the feature and you will find the control.

above THE CONTROL DESCRIPTION SHEET WILL LET YOU KNOW WHERE TO LOOK FOR THE MARKER ONCE YOU HAVE LOCATED THE CONTROL FEATURE. HERE, THE BOULDER MAKES A BIG DIFFERENCE, AND KNOWING THAT THE MARKER IS IN FACT ON TOP OF THE BOULDER MAKES FINDING IT MUCH EASIER.

Basic pitfalls in navigation (and how to avoid them)

Navigational errors tend to increase as the competitor picks up speed and also as he or she becomes more tired. As such, mistakes are more likely to occur if the orienteer is trying to navigate at high speed or near the end of a course. Here are some of the most common errors that orienteers make:

Following another orienteer

Orienteers soon learn that following other competitors, as well as being strictly against the rules can also lead to problems. Firstly, you can never be sure that the other person is on the same course as you are. Secondly, even if he is, he may not be going in the right direction.

Even if you find an orienteer who is on your course and going in the right direction it is unwise to blindly follow him. Should you subsequently lose him and you were not navigating, you will be unsure of your own location.

Being drawn by an incorrect control or the wrong feature

In an event where many control points are used, you may see other markers which are not your specific one. Since you are unable to see the control code from a distance, the temptation is to go and look 'just in case' it is the marker you are looking for. Rather stick to the map and your navigation skills. Check to see if the control is where it should be and if not, ignore it, as it is likely to be the wrong one.

You may also see a feature which appears to be the correct one. You should take great care in an area that has lots of features, and use the map to fine-navigate into the correct control. Try to avoid seeing a feature, thinking that it must be the one and heading for it while ignoring the surrounding features.

180° error

When using the compass to take a bearing, you must ensure that the red arrow on the compass housing points north along the magnetic north lines depicted on the map.

If you are taking a bearing in the center of the map, the magnetic north lines will be obvious, but which direction north is may not be.

Similarly, when the compass is taken off the map, the red end of the needle must be pointing in the same direction as the red arrow on the compass housing.

If you get either of these wrong, you will end up going in exactly the opposite direction to the intended one. This is called a 180° error. While this may sound unlikely in theory, the fact remains that it does happen in practice, especially if bearings are taken in a hurry or if the competitor is tired.

The solution is to exercise great care when taking compass bearings, but also to check the map carefully. In this case, you should be able to pick up fairly quickly that you are going in the wrong direction.

90° error

This happens most often when there is a path or ride system in the area, which occurs on a grid system. On arriving at a junction from the forest, the competitor takes the wrong path and ends up going east instead of north or west instead of south. Again, this may sound unlikely, but it happens, and is known as the 90° error.

To avoid this type of error you should regularly check the bearing of the path that you are on. Comparing this to the bearing of the correct path depicted on the map should give an early warning that the incorrect route has been taken.

Parallel error

Unlike the 180° and 90° errors, the parallel error is the most difficult to detect in practice and can lead to much frustration and time lost during competition.

You could end up on a feature or in an area which is similar to the one that you expect to be at, but is in actual fact the wrong place — everything seems to fit except that the control marker cannot be found.

Even if the area is not identical to the one where you should be, you convince yourself that you are in the right place and attempt to make everything fit according to the map. The secret to overcoming this error is to break this train of thought and admit the possibility that you could be in the wrong place after all. It is then a matter of relocating and finding a point that leaves absolutely no doubt as to where you are on the map. This may be difficult if there are no such points close to the control marker.

Looking too soon

If distance estimation is not good, the orienteer may slow down and start looking for the control too soon. Depending on the area and the route chosen, this may be up to several hundred meters before the correct spot.

If the competitor keeps on going in the same direction until he finds the correct area, the only problem is a loss of time. However, if he starts searching the wrong area more thoroughly for the checkpoint then a significant amount of time can be lost and frustration sets in. The best solution is to find an attack point relatively close to the control — the shorter the distance between the two, the better, as there is less chance of an error in the distance estimation.

Overshooting

Similarly, a competitor may run well past the area where the control is and only then start searching for it. Distance judgment and use of correct attack points are the best means of reducing this type of error.

MAKING USE OF A CATCHING FEATURE WILL REDUCE THE RISK OF OVERSHOOTING A CONTROL.

Another option is to look for features that you would expect to find beyond the control. There may be an obvious catching feature and if this is reached you will know that you have gone too far. If it is a line feature, such as a path or stream, it will be easier to see and use; but point features, such as a knoll or boulder, can also be used in this way.

Ignoring the compass

Although it is true that on occasion the compass can give an incorrect reading, the chances are that the compass is correct. It is therefore essential to take note of the direction in which you are heading all the time. If the path is supposed to run north–south and the compass tells you it is actually running northeast–southwest, chances are that you are on the wrong path. Use the compass regularly; ignore it at your peril!

Relying on the compass too much

Having said that, it is possible to put too much trust in the compass. Setting a bearing and running on that bearing for 500m (550yd) without reading the map can lead to trouble. Given the error that can occur with following a bearing and distance estimate, you could end up anywhere within a 50m (55yd) radius of your correct destination. While this does not sound like a lot, it can be, particularly if the terrain is steep, the vegetation thick or the visibility poor.

Using the map in conjunction with the compass will reduce this error and ensure that your position at the end of 500m (550yd) is much more accurate than by using the compass alone.

Reading too much detail on the map

Although the detail shown on the map is important close to a control, much of the detail can be ignored while running between controls.

If you have to travel 500m (550yd) in a northerly direction through the forest from one track to the next, the detail in that forest is largely irrelevant. At best you may want to mentally check that everything looks correct — ensuring that everything is exactly where it should be would only waste valuable time.

Help! I don't know where I am

Sooner or later all orienteers get lost. One of the differences between top class orienteers and newcomers is the ability to relocate easily. This is one of the most important techniques in orienteering. Unfortunately the only real way to learn to relocate better is to practice — and that means getting lost.

It is important to distinguish between not knowing exactly where you are and being totally lost. Generally you will have some idea of where you are. If you are in between controls on a compass bearing but the ground doesn't seem to fit the map, the first thing to do is check your bearing. If this is correct, the best option is to keep going in the hope that you will come across a feature that you do recognize. If there is a nearby line feature, it may be worth deviating from the direct route to reconfirm your position.

If you are not on a straight-line route, it is best to try to relocate. Ensure that the map is aligned and try to pick out some obvious features to assist you. Failing this, you should head in a particular direction, where you know there should be a recognizable feature (usually a line feature) that will allow you to relocate.

Should you become lost in the vicinity of the control, the worst thing you can do is wander around in circles. You may be lucky and find the control but chances are that you won't. If aligning the map and trying to fit the features on the ground to it fails to determine your location, then the best thing is to head out to a suitable attack point.

If you become totally lost the only option is to set a bearing in the direction of where you believe a line feature will be and head in that direction.

Relocating is not an easy task, but it is an important skill to acquire. The better your map reading skills, the better you will become at relocating.

Relocation

- When alarm bells ring, STOP, LOOK and LISTEN.
- Try to remember where you were on the map the last time you were certain of your position.
- Orientate the map.
- How far have you come, and what have you passed?
- Look around you. Try to find a large or clear feature to identify on the ground and on the map.
- Note its relationship to other, smaller features.
- Have you made a parallel error?
- What other mistake could you have made?
- If you cannot determine where you are, take a compass bearing to a large line feature, for example, a field edge or road, noting your direction of travel and any significant terrain details.
- If you are still lost, retrace your steps to the last point at which you can be certain of your position, even if this means the previous control.

GETTING TO GRIPS WITH THE BASIC PRINCIPLES OF RELOCATION WILL HELP YOU GET BACK ON TRACK.

Basic Training

Strategy in orienteering is not complicated, but proper preparation and training is very important even before you start the race.

An orienteer's training will be divided into three equally important parts. Physical training, technical training and mental preparation.

Training the body

Physical training for orienteering and the related fitness level is different from any other sport. The competitor must be able to run through rough terrain at high speed. As well as basic leg speed, the competitor needs to have stamina and the ability to maintain concentration throughout the race — most mistakes occur when an orienteer is tired.

A course may include path running, rocky areas, marshes, open moorland, forests and thick undergrowth. Due to the huge variation in types of terrain, the speed of the competitor will vary greatly over the different types of ground. Thus learning to run at one speed on one type of terrain is not going to help with orienteering fitness.

For this reason, **fartlek** (Swedish for 'speed play') plays a big role in orienteering fitness training. Simply put, this means doing a run, preferably in orienteering terrain, where the speed is varied according to the type of terrain and the physical effort required to cross it. Fartlek takes away the monotony of structured speed-work and makes it varied and more enjoyable. As such you can apply your fastest speed when running on a path downhill and your slowest going uphill through thick undergrowth, with different speeds in-between.

Other forms of physical training include:

Long slow runs — Slower than race pace, these runs will help to build stamina. Runs will generally be up to 50 per cent longer than your typical racing distance and should preferably be done in orienteering terrain. If conditions do not allow this, running on the road or even on a treadmill is better than not running at all.

Faster runs — Shorter training sessions are carried out at a faster pace in order to improve speed. Both the long run and fast run are best done in groups but can also be done alone.

Time trials — A specific distance (e.g. 8km; 5 miles) is run as fast as possible in order to build speed. You can benefit from running at a similar speed with others who 'compete' against you and thus ensure fast times. Many time trial courses have the kilometer markers indicated so that progress can be measured throughout the session.

Interval training — Probably the hardest type of training, interval training involves running flat-out over set distances followed by short recovery periods. Thus an interval session might consist of 20x200m (220yd) flat-out with 20 seconds rest between each; 10x400m (440yd) with 45 seconds rest between each; or 6x800m (880yd) with 90 seconds rest between each.

Interval training is normally carried out on a track or road and warming up is essential to avoid possible injury. Since orienteering is an endurance event, 800m intervals are probably the best.

Hill running — This constitutes a specific type of interval training. Find a hill which is not too steep, ideally some 200–400m (650–1300ft) in incline. After warming up, run up the hill as hard as you can and then

> **opposite** A GOOD FITNESS PROGRAMME WILL INCLUDE VARIETY IN TERMS OF PHYSICAL TRAINING AND TERRAIN.

jog down. Start off with five repetitions and build up to 10, 15 or 20 repetitions over a period of time. Hill running will build leg strength and also help when climbing 'real' hills on an orienteering course.

Cross training — Practice another sport apart from running. Many orienteers use cross training as a change from the usual training routine to add variety.

Other sports can also build different muscles. However, remember to use other sports only to offer a variation from orienteering training and not as the main form of training.

Train in similar terrain — Some large events actually offer training events prior to the main competition. For major events such as the World Championships, teams hold training camps in similar terrain close to the competition area so that participants can familiarize themselves with the type of terrain that they will be competing in.

It is important to get to grips with the terrain beforehand, if you can, as you don't want to spend precious moments during the race doing precisely that.

Strength training — Usually takes the form of a series of exercises in the gym. These could include push-ups, sit-ups, step-ups, abdominal crunches, skipping and weights. Your local gym should be able to devise a suitable training circuit for you.

Stretching — To run over the rough terrain that you will encounter at most events, your limbs need to be supple. As a result, stretching is extremely important for orienteers — it is advisable to stretch before and after an event to avoid possible injury.

A typical warm-up routine will consist of general loosening, walking or jogging and static stretching. Gentle loosening exercises could include ankle rotations, heel raises, hip rotations and spinal rotations. The amount of jogging required will depend on your fitness level and how fast you intend to run the course.

Static stretching could include an upper body stretch, calf stretch, calf and Achilles tendon stretch, inner thigh stretch, hamstring stretch and quadriceps stretch. Remember, every body is different and each orienteer should develop his own warm-up routine. See opposite for a recommended stretching routine.

Stretching routine

A STRETCH YOUR RIGHT ARM ACROSS YOUR CHEST AND PLACING YOUR LEFT HAND JUST ABOVE THE ELBOW, TUG GENTLY TOWARDS YOU AND HOLD FOR A FEW SECONDS. REPEAT WITH THE OTHER ARM.

B STANDING UPRIGHT, WITH YOUR HIPS FACING FORWARD AND FEET SPREAD SLIGHTLY APART, GENTLY EXTEND ONE HAND DOWN TO KNEE-LEVEL, THEN THE OTHER. DROP YOUR NECK TOWARDS YOUR SHOULDERS AS YOU DO THIS; FEEL THE STRETCH IN YOUR OPPOSITE SIDE.

C FOR A GOOD UPPER BODY STRETCH, CLASP YOUR HANDS BEHIND YOUR BACK AND HOLD FOR A FEW SECONDS. THIS EXPANDS THE CHEST AND LOOSENS THE SHOULDER JOINTS, INCREASING FLEXIBILITY.

D STANDING UPRIGHT WITH YOUR FEET PLACED SLIGHTLY APART, BEND ONE LEG INTO A CROUCHING POSTION AND STRETCH THE OTHER LEG OUT TO THE SIDE UNTIL YOU FEEL TENSION IN THE ADDUCTORS. HOLD FOR A FEW SECONDS, THEN REPEAT WITH THE OTHER LEG.

E STANDING UPRIGHT, CROSS YOUR LEGS AT THE ANKLES, THEN BEND FORWARD AT THE WAIST AND GRAB YOUR ANKLES OR TOUCH THE FLOOR AS BEST YOU CAN UNTIL YOU FEEL THE TENSION IN YOUR HAMSTRINGS. RECROSS YOUR LEGS, PLACING THE OPPOSITE FOOT IN FRONT AND REPEAT.

F STEP FORWARD INTO A HALF LUNGE, KEEPING THE BACK STRAIGHT. HOLD FOR A FEW SECONDS UNTIL YOU FEEL THE STRETCH IN

YOUR QUADRICEPS THEN SLOWLY STRAIGHTEN UP. REPEAT WITH THE OTHER LEG. FOR A MORE INTENSE WORKOUT TRY BALANCING A SUITABLY WEIGHTED BARBELL ON YOUR SHOULDERS.

G LIE ON THE FLOOR WITH BOTH LEGS OUTSTRETCHED. BEND ONE LEG AT THE KNEE, HOOK YOUR HANDS BEHIND THE KNEE AND PULL TOWARDS YOUR CHEST UNTIL YOU FEEL TENSION IN YOUR HAMSTRING. REPEAT WITH THE OTHER LEG.

H STAND HALF AN ARM'S LENGTH FROM A WALL, WITH ONE FOOT A SHORT DISTANCE IN FRONT OF THE OTHER. BEND THE FRONT LEG SLIGHTLY AND STRETCH THE BACK LEG OUT BEHIND YOU UNTIL YOU FEEL TENSION IN THE LOWER CALF AND ACHILLES TENDON.

Nutrition

As you become more competitive and regularly take part in events, the correct nutrition will form an important part of your training. To be able to perform at the highest level you will require not only a fit body and trained eye, but also increased vitality and energy.

Three food groups are essential in providing the body with energy and the ability to build and repair muscle: carbohydrates, proteins and fats.

Carbohydrates

Carbohydrates are digested and broken down into glucose, and stored in the muscles as glycogen, which in turn supplies the body with its most accessible source of energy.

Complex carbohydrates, such as pasta, potatoes, bananas and rye bread provide the most sustained form of energy, and for this reason many athletes will 'carbo-load' before a strenuous event, i.e. store as much energy in their muscles as possible two to three days before the competition. Because the body can only convert glucose to glycogen (the body's fuel) at a certain rate, it is preferable to eat a number of smaller meals throughout the day than one large one. If the body is bombarded with glucose, it will convert only a given amount to glycogen and store the remainder as fat.

A typical carbo-loading day could include the following three meals:

Breakfast
Oat porridge with sugar and milk
Rye toast with honey or jam
Sweetened tea or coffee

Lunch
Jacket potato with a cheese filling
Fresh fruit, such as bananas, for dessert

Dinner
Pasta with a simple meat or tomato sauce
Rice pudding or dried fruit for dessert

Proteins

Protein-rich foods are an important source of amino acids. Meat, chicken, fish, beans, grains and legumes not only help to supplement the body's own amino acids, they also supply the six amino acids that the body cannot produce itself. Amino acids are essential as they are the building blocks that facilitate rebuilding and repair after exercise.

Fats

Although, fats are a highly concentrated source of energy, providing more energy than carbohydrates, they are more slow-releasing. It is only with continuous exercise, once the body's glycogen energy sources are depleted, that the body gradually begins to metabolize fat as an alternate source of fuel.

Although a moderate amount of fat is essential to any diet, it is also important to be aware of the dangers of consuming too much, such as high cholesterol levels and weight gain. It is advisable to stay away from saturated fats, such as animal fats, coconut and palm oil, as these have a high cholesterol content. A high level of cholesterol in the blood can clog arteries and, in some cases, lead to heart disease. Consume instead products such as avocados and nuts, which provide the body with monounsaturated fats, considered 'good' cholesterol as they carry fat deposits from arteries to the liver for excretion.

Water

About 75 per cent of the body consists of water. As a sportsperson it is advisable to consume a substantial amount of water (about eight to 14 glasses) every day. Avoid fizzy or caffeinated drinks as they limit the absorption of certain nutrients.

Recovery

Once you have taken part in an event, it is important to rest your muscles and replenish your body's energy levels. You should return to a balanced, healthy and nutritional diet and continue to exercise, but reduce the intensity of your workouts.

Training program

Like other sports, the training program for orienteers can be divided into four distinct parts:

1. The competitor must establish a base fitness. This is usually done during the off-season and will consist of building up base mileage. During winter, when the days are shorter and competitors are unable to train outdoors during daylight hours, many orienteers will take advantage of the local gym to build up their stamina.

2. The orienteer will increase the level of training in order to build up to a specific competition. The quantity of training may decrease, but the quality will increase, with an emphasis on improving speed and building stamina. Training sessions will include hill training to build strength and faster runs, fartlek and interval training to improve speed.

3. During the competition phase, the main effort will be focused on actual event days but training will still be carried out on other days. This, however, must be lighter and not detract from the main aim of this period, which is to do well in competitions. Rest is an important part of the racing phase; it is important that you are not tired going into a race.

4. The competition phase will be followed by a recovery phase during which the orienteer will reduce the training load and allow the body to recover. It is important, however, to keep training otherwise all the hard work that has gone into the previous three phases will be lost.

Phases two, three and four may be repeated twice if the competitor must peak for two major events during the year. Trying to achieve peak fitness more than twice per year is extremely difficult and not normally attempted, so it is important to select one or two major events during the year that will be the focus of the training program.

Please note: As a recreational orienteer, wishing to sustain or improve an ordinary level of fitness for competitions around the year, you should tailor training programs and nutrition to suit your specific needs.

How much should I train?

This is a difficult question to answer and will depend on the individual as much as the set objective. During the second phase of training, which will probably involve the most work, top orienteers will be covering 80–120km (50–75 miles) per week.

The key is never to push your body too far. Never train if you are feeling under the weather or tired from a previous training session. Listen to your body — it will tell you whether you are doing too much.

On reaching the competition phase, the quantity of training will reduce but the quality will increase, as will the switch from non-orienteering terrain to orienteering terrain.

Many top competitors will train twice a day, particularly in the build-up phase. However, one important rule to remember when developing a training program is not to increase the amount too quickly. Experts recommend no more than a 10 per cent increase in mileage per week. This will reduce the risk of injury.

 Fitness warning

One warning on the effects of improved fitness: some competitors find that as they get fitter their actual orienteering performance deteriorates. Strange as this may seem, it is because the orienteer is now able to run faster than he can navigate. He no longer has the time to navigate properly and therefore makes more mistakes. The only way to avoid this is to improve the speed of navigation at the same time. Thus it is important not just to focus on physical training but also on technical training.

Whereas runners can gauge their fitness by timing a run over a specific distance, this is difficult for orienteers due to the variety of terrains they race in. Try setting up a short 3–5km (2–3 miles) training course in a local orienteering area, using as many different types of terrain as possible. Run this at top speed at regular intervals to see if your orienteering fitness is improving.

ALL THE HARD WORK SEEMS WORTHWHILE WHEN YOU ACHIEVE YOUR GOALS — THESE YOUNG WOMEN CELEBRATE THEIR WIN AT THE WORLD CHAMPIONSHIPS.

Training the eye

Technical training is required to improve map reading, ground interpretation, control finding, route choice and general navigation skills. This essentially involves training the eye in order to be able to identify the relevant amount of detail on a map and match it up to the corresponding detail on the ground.

As you become more confident, you will find it easier to pick out the most important features. The following exercises will help you to improve in these areas:

Technical training

Compass work and distance work

Set a course with controls on features about 100–300m (110–330yd) apart (this exercise works best in areas that are relatively flat with not too many features). Then use accurate compass work and pacing to visit the controls. This develops the skill of finding controls from an attack point in similar areas, i.e. flat and featureless.

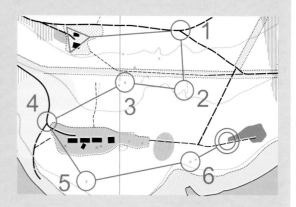

Contour interpretation

This exercise needs to be carried out in an area of high contour detail. Several controls are placed in the area, again 100–300m (110–330yd) apart. A course is then set and the orienteer uses fine navigation skills, relying particularly on the contours, to locate the controls.

The exercise is further improved if a 'contour only' map of the area can be obtained. With no other detail on the map, the orienteer must rely solely on the contours for navigation.

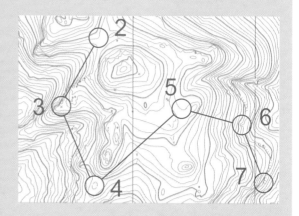

Line orienteering

Another exercise that improves navigation skills involves drawing a line on the map. Several controls are placed on features cut by this line. The idea is for you to follow the line and find the location of the controls which you then mark on the map. Obviously you must follow the line very carefully or you may miss one of the controls.

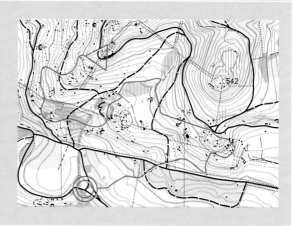

Window orienteering

For this exercise, only a 'window' of approximately 100m (110yd) in diameter around each control is shown, with the rest of the map blanked out. You are thus reliant on the compass to get you from one window to the next. Once you arrive in the window area you can use the map detail to locate the control. This exercise will teach rough compass navigation skills.

Controls can be placed quite far apart in this exercise; the further apart they are, the bigger the window should be to allow for error on the rough compass leg. However, there must be no hidden obstacles between the controls that will impede direct line progress.

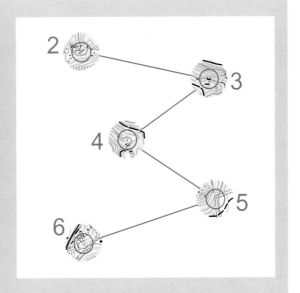

Corridor orienteering

This involves navigating around a course where all of the map is blocked out except for a narrow corridor along the direct route between the controls. Thus, like line orienteering, you must navigate along the corridor. Straying to either side you run the risk of getting lost with no map to aid navigation.

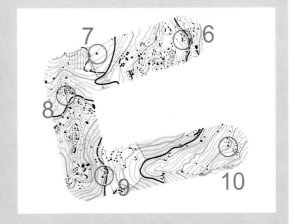

Armchair orienteering

It may appear to be the lazy orienteer's way of training but in fact looking at maps, courses and route choices can be very beneficial.

You should choose a map with a course on it and then study the route choices available for each leg. Since it is not possible to actually check out the route on the ground, it is best to discuss the route with other orienteers and see if they agree with your choice. They may have seen a route that you had not thought of.

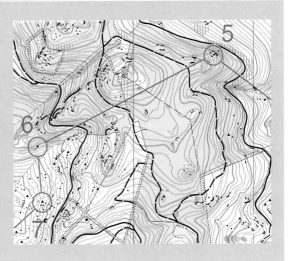

Shadowing

Shadowing is when two orienteers train together with one following to watch how the other navigates. On arrival at each control the two can discuss the route taken and whether any improvement could have been made. If the follower is coaching the leader, the exercise continues around a series of controls. If the orienteers are learning from each other, they can change over for the next leg so that the leader becomes the follower and vice versa.

Relocation training

A variation on shadowing is for only the leader to carry a map. The follower must, however, try to remember the features that they come across after leaving the previous control. Halfway through the leg, the leader hands the map to the follower who has to try to 'relocate', i.e. find out where they are on the map and complete the leg.

This can also be done when you have arrived within 100m (110yd) of the control marker. Not only will you learn relocation skills but control location skills will also be developed.

Reading the map on the run

Learning to read the map on the run can save a lot of time during a competition and is an essential skill for any aspiring orienteer. Most newcomers will spend a considerable amount of time standing still, reading the map. While this should ensure that the map is read correctly it also wastes a lot of time. Top orienteers will hardly ever stand still as they have learned to read the map on the run, even in complex terrain.

This skill can be developed by simply running with the map in hand. The map should have a course marked on it and you should read the map as you would while actually doing the course, taking in all the features and detail required to navigate around it.

It takes some imagination but it is an excellent way of learning to read the map while 'in motion'. Best practiced in an orienteering area, this skill can also be developed by running along a straight stretch of similar terrain.

Map memory

This involves running around a course without a map! At each control there is a small piece of map showing the next leg of the course. The orienteer must then remember where the next control, the selected route and the relevant features along that route are located.

Complex areas (and complex legs) can provide great challenges and also help to develop map interpretation and route choice skills, which will be invaluable in competition.

Quick thinking

Two exercises that will help to save time on an orienteering course are master map copying and control punching:

Master map copying

When copying your course from a master map to your own map, accuracy is essential. Every orienteer at some time or another has copied a circle in the wrong place only to lose time when searching for the control or perhaps not finding it at all.

However, copying the course quickly but accurately can save precious minutes, depending on the number of controls to be copied. This exercise can be practiced at home when getting out is difficult.

Control punching

If there are 20 controls on your course and you spend 30 seconds at each one, that is 10 minutes wasted just punching controls! Even 10 seconds per control is over three minutes. It is therefore important to be able to check the code and punch the card (*see* p57) quickly and correctly at each control.

This is best accomplished by having the control card attached to your wrist, leaving it readily available for punching. On approaching a control, you should know the code so that you can quickly confirm that you are in the correct place. You should also already know which

direction you will be leaving the control. This is important not only to avoid wasting time but also to ensure that you do not inadvertently advertise the location of the control to another competitor by standing next to it for too long.

Putting out a number of controls (you can even do this in your garden) and seeing how fast you can punch them all will improve your skill in this respect. Electronic punching is much faster than the manual method, but regardless of the system, efficient punching can save vital seconds which may mean the difference between winning or losing, particularly in a short race.

Getting the code right

Each control marker has a code marked on it. This can be a combination of numbers and/or letters but is most often a three-digit number.

This code is indicated on the control description sheet. It is important for the competitor to check that the control which has been located has the correct code marked on it. In large competitions with a greater number of controls it is easy to come across the wrong control — the code will confirm whether the correct control marker has actually been found.

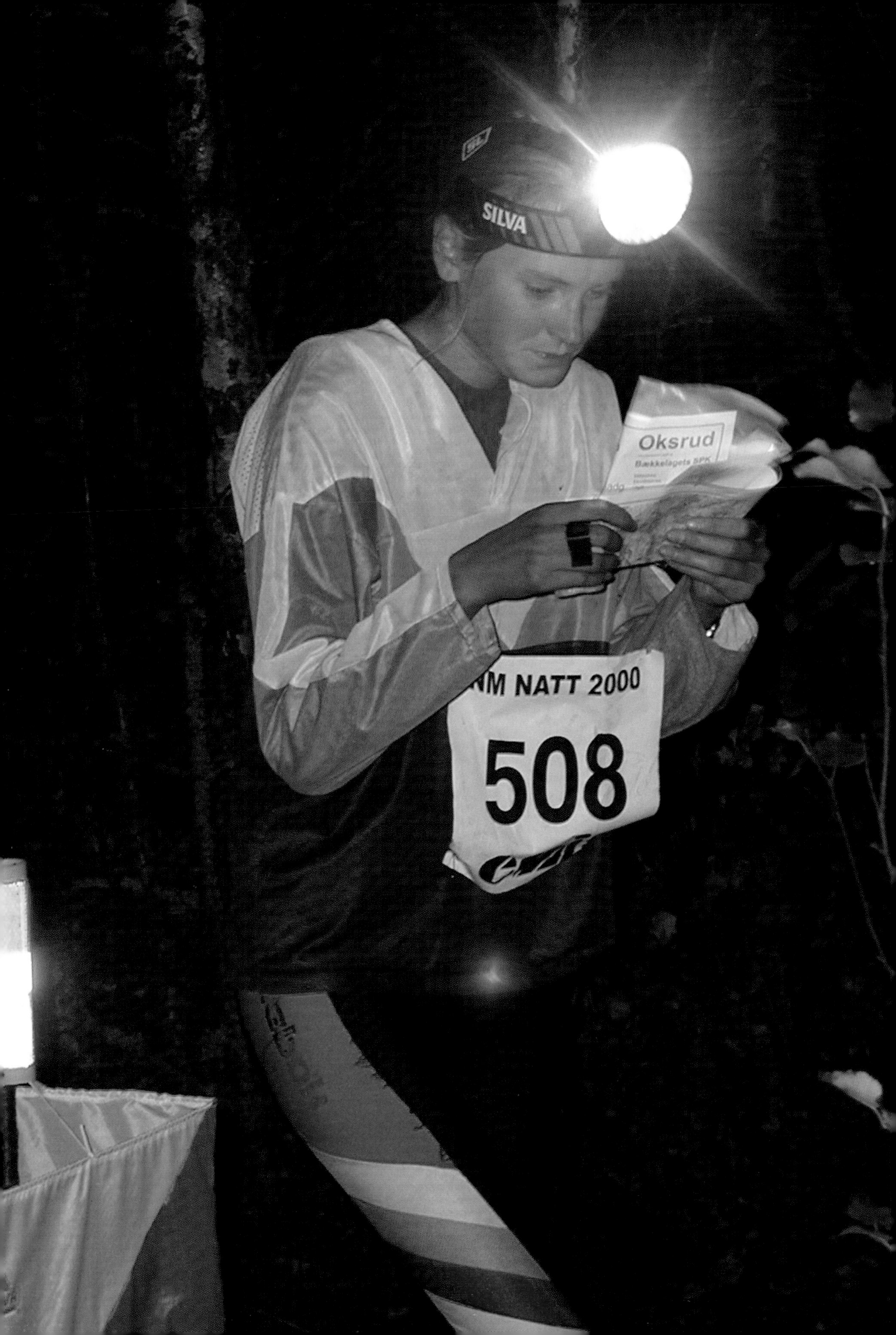
SILVA
Oksrud
Bækkelagets SPK
NM NATT 2000
508

The mental game

Success at the highest level of sport these days is not just about fitness and skill. It is also about your mental ability to cope with the pressure. Orienteering is no different and, in fact, if your mental approach is not right then no amount of training is going to get you to the top.

One essential skill to learn is concentration. Most mistakes are made when concentration is broken, either due to an outside influence (seeing another competitor or being attracted by an incorrect control) or by internal factors such as tiredness.

Unfortunately, there is no easy way of improving concentration, but the following may help:

Ignore other competitors

Although some competitors may be on the same course or looking for the same control, experience has taught that it is best to 'do your own thing'. If you see other people, try to ignore them and concentrate on your own navigation to find the control.

Follow a routine

Aim to have a set routine before a race. This should ensure that you have all the correct equipment, all the information available about the course and that you are correctly warmed up. It also means that you will arrive at the start in the right frame of mind, fully focused on the course ahead. Try to avoid distractions ahead of a race and ensure that you arrive in plenty of time so that your preparation does not have to be rushed.

Avoid early mistakes

It is very important to get off to a good start on an orienteering course. Thus being extra careful on the first leg is generally a good idea. It also allows you to warm up (if this has not been properly done beforehand) and to get a good idea of the terrain and the map.

opposite NO MATTER HOW GOOD YOU ARE AT NAVIGATING OR MAP READING, A LAPSE IN CONCENTRATION COULD AFFECT YOUR RUN.

Put mistakes behind you

Mistakes do happen and time will inevitably be lost. Very few runs are perfect. If you make a mistake on one leg, you need to be able to put it behind you straight away. Focus on the next leg and those that follow and try to forget the problem leg. What's done is done and worrying about it may only lead to further mistakes.

Don't psych yourself out

Sometimes when looking at a leg, you think, 'This is going to be tricky'. By approaching it in this frame of mind, the chances are that it will turn out to be a problem. Always try to be positive. Analyze the leg and use your navigation skills to select a route choice with an appropriate attack point. Rarely will a leg be so difficult that there is not a logical way of approaching it.

Motivation/setting goals

Plan your season. Decide which races you want to peak for. Plan your training around these major events and use other events as training. If you have goals, at whatever level you compete, you are much more likely to be motivated and therefore much more likely to succeed.

Self-confidence

Nothing succeeds like success. It is therefore very important to be confident when going into a race. The feeling of finding a control exactly where you think it should be is great. Having the confidence to navigate correctly often means that you will. It is very important to believe in yourself as this is often the difference between a good performance and a poor one.

Whereas fitness and technical skills can be improved relatively easily, mental stamina is something that only comes with experience. Joining a club and finding a coach are two ways to make this process easier. However, at the end of the day, trying things out and seeing what works best for you is the only real way of developing these skills.

Post-race analysis

One important method for improving your orienteering ability is the post-race analysis. Perhaps more than any other sport it is important to analyze the course you have just completed, look at the mistakes you made and try to learn from them.

Using the chart below, take time after an event to review your performance together with some of the following guidelines:

1. Draw the route that you took on the map. If there are any instances where you are unsure of the exact route you took indicate this on the map.

2. Write down the split times for each leg between controls. A useful tool in this regard is the sports watch which is able to record split times at each control. Split times are provided if electronic punching is used.

3. Write a description of the route you took between each control and why you selected that route.

4. Include any problems you had or mistakes that you might have made.

5. Calculate the speed between each control. You must allow for any climbing on the leg — it is usual to count a 10m (30ft) vertical climb as 100m (110yd) distance.

$$\text{Thus:} \quad \text{Speed (min/km)} = \frac{\text{Time (min)}}{\text{Distance (km)} + \text{Climb (m)} \times 10}$$

6. Analyze the mistakes you made on each leg and estimate the time lost.

7. If you can discuss your route with competitors who ran the same course, then so much the better. Compare routes, compare times and see how you might have followed a better route or confirm that you took the best route.

Event analysis chart

Mistake	Minutes lost on each leg									
	1	2	3	4	5	6	7	8	9	10
1. Not choosing proper attack point										
2. Poor route choice										
3. Not looking at the map with enough care:										
a) leaving control										
b) going into a control										
4. Should have planned ahead										
5. Not checking the compass										
a) leaving control										
b) reaching track, stream, etc.										
6. Taking time to run accurately when rough bearing would do										
7. Using wrong map feature										
8. Not careful enough from attack point										
9. Not running accurately on bearing										
10. Deliberate risk didn't work										
11. No recovery plan after missing control										
12. Loss of concentration										
13. Not pace counting										
TOTAL TIME LOST										

Punching devices

There are currently two types of punching devices in use at major orienteering events:

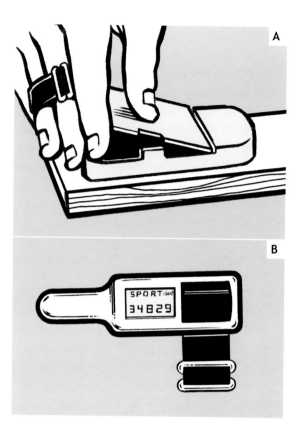

A EMIT — The EMIT device makes use of a credit card size 'card' about 3mm in thickness. The card is placed into a recessed slot on the punching device located at each control. The 'E card' (as it is called) has a loop of elastic at one end, similar to a luggage tag, which fits around the competitor's finger. A piece of thin card is attached to the other side of the card, and a mark is made on this when the card is correctly inserted into the slot. The marks are used as back-up should the electronic system fail for any reason.

B SPORTident — This device is cylindrical in shape, about 5cm (2in) in length and 1cm (½in) in diameter. It is also attached to the competitor's finger with an elastic loop. At each control, the end of the device must be insterted into a hole. With this system an audible tone indicates that the device has registered the visit.

Recording split times

A split time is the time taken between any two given points on part of the course — usually the time taken between controls. There are digital watches available that contain memory to record consecutive split times. However, the electronic punching systems used these days (EMIT or SPORTident) also record the time taken between each control.

By recording your split times you can determine how you fared on each leg; you can even compare your split times with those run by other competitors and determine how far behind the fastest competitor you were.

At large international events where electronic punching is used, a competitor's split times will be recorded and displayed on the organizer's website. The winner's times and route choice will also be published to aid you in your post-race analysis.

AT MOST LARGE EVENTS ELECTRONIC PUNCHING DEVICES ARE USED TO RECORD YOUR VISIT TO A CONTROL.

Competitive Orienteering

Orienteering can be enjoyed as a social sport and at a recreational level. However, it can also be practiced at the highest international level with World Championships. Most orienteering countries hold annual national and regional championships and many have badge schemes which enable competitors to assess their own skill and work towards a higher level of competition.

Virtually all competitive orienteers will join a club. This offers many benefits including regular information about events. Many clubs also hold club events and training sessions for their members. Not only is training with a group more fun, you will also learn a lot from more experienced orienteers. Membership of a club and the regional/national association is usually a prerequisite for competing in regional and national championships.

To find out when an event will be taking place near you, contact your local orienteering club or national orienteering federation. These days, there is also a lot of information available on the Internet.

Make sure you can go the distance

A word of warning: the length of orienteering courses is deceptive. Many newcomers have looked at a 3–4km (2–2½ mile) course and thought the distance far too short and far too easy, especially if they are fit and used to running longer distances.

Always start with the shortest course or, at the very least, the second shortest. If you complete that easily and quickly, you can always attempt a longer, more difficult course the next time. When newcomers make the mistake of underestimating the difficulty of the sport and attempt courses way beyond their ability, they are disillusioned because they don't finish or take hours to complete a 5km (3-mile) course, and never return.

It is wise to obtain information about an event well in advance. A local event may cater for a mere handful of people while the biggest event in the world, the Swedish five-day O-Ringen which takes place annually in July, often attracts more than 20,000 avid orienteers.

It is also important to determine what type of event is being held and whether you need to pre-enter. Many big events require that you enter weeks or even months in advance, and distribute entry forms for this purpose. However, most will offer entry-on-the-day courses which are especially useful for beginners.

Levels of events

As mentioned in the introduction, orienteering is an ideal family sport as events cater for all abilities and age groups. Both experienced orienteers and newcomers can therefore attend most orienteering events and select the level of competition they wish to attempt.

Come-and-try-it (CATI) events are aimed purely at beginners and newcomers. One or more short, easy courses (1–3km; ½–2 miles) are provided, offering an excellent basic introduction to the sport. Experienced orienteers are generally on hand to give a quick lesson in basic map reading skills, and the navigation required to complete the courses is generally very simple — usually a compass would not be necessary at such an event.

CATI events cater for groups as well as individuals. However, to really benefit from the orienteering experience it is recommended that groups be no larger than three people. Indeed, when there are three different opinions as to the correct way to go, many people will understand why most orienteers prefer to go it alone!

opposite ONCE YOU'RE HOOKED, YOU'LL LIVE FOR THE COMPETITION.

Your first event

The prospect of your first event can seem daunting, but don't be discouraged! If you've done all your training the race itself should not present a problem, and there will be experienced orienteers available to assist you with route choice and give you basic tips on orienteering.

Once you arrive at the event, head for registration. Officials here will provide you with information about the courses on offer and how long and difficult they are.

1

Study the map carefully. What scale is it? Do you understand the symbols? Look at the overall picture of the terrain — what are the main types of features? Much useful information can be obtained by this procedure. Most maps include the legend. If not, and you are not sure what a symbol means, seek assistance.

At events with pre-marked maps you will only receive your map at the start. However, blank maps may be available near registration and it is advisable to study one of these.

4

Competitors are called a few minutes before their actual start time. Follow the tapes to the master maps and copy down the course onto your blank map. Number the controls and join them up in order. Be sure to mark all the controls and the location of the start (triangle) and finish (double circle). It is worth taking some time to ensure that the circles are marked accurately as incorrectly marked controls may be impossible to find.

Go at your own pace and ignore your fellow competitors. Visit all the controls in the correct order, making sure to record your visit by punching your control card. Each control marker has a different identification code. The control description sheet will give you the codes and locations of controls.

7

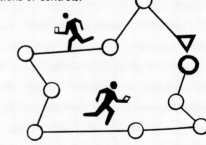

8

After paying your entry fee, you will be invited to select a course suited to your age, experience and skill level.

You will receive a map, a control card and a description sheet. Make a note of your start time, which will be written on your control card.

2

3

Study the control description sheet. This will tell you how many controls there are on the course. For each checkpoint it will also indicate the description of the feature you are looking for and its identifying code.

On beginner courses the descriptions will usually be given in words. However, on courses for experienced orienteers, the international control descriptions will be used. You will need to familiarize yourself with these as you graduate to these courses (see Appendix A).

5

You must write your name, club and category (course or age group) on your control card. The card consists of a series of numbered boxes, which you will punch at each control visited. Each control has a different needle punch, which produces a unique pattern on your control card. This will let the organizers know that you have visited the correct checkpoint.

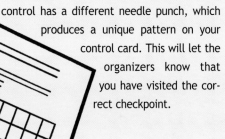

6

Once you have punched the last control proceed to the finish and hand in your control card.

9

Your card will be checked to see that you have been to the correct controls and your time will be calculated. Results will be displayed according to course category and time on the results line or board.

10

Color-coded (or Club) events are probably the most common type of event in many countries. A variety of courses with increasing difficulty, ranging from 1–3km (½–2 miles) upwards in length, are available for beginners to experienced orienteers. The courses are usually described in terms of physical difficulty (easy, medium, hard) and navigational difficulty (beginner, more experienced, experienced, very experienced).

In an attempt to standardize these difficulty levels between events, some countries have adopted a color-coding system with each color representing a certain physical and navigational difficulty. This system makes it much easier for competitors to select the appropriate course for their level and gauge their improvement over a number of events.

Groups are also generally welcome at Club events, especially on the shorter courses. However, the longer courses may preclude groups and generally where ranking points are awarded to competitors, groups do not qualify.

National or Ranking events represent the next level up. Whereas CATI and Club events mainly run the courses on orienteering experience and ability, National events have age group categories. These will vary from country to country but in general the official IOF age group categories are used (*see* Appendix D).

Often there will be more than one course per age category. Thus there may be an M40 (Men's 40) Long and an M40 Short course. For these, the navigational difficulty will be similar but the length of the course will vary.

Sometimes A, B and C courses are offered (E, for 'Elite', only at major events). The B course will not only be shorter but technically easier than the A course. Similarly, the C course will be physically and technically easier still. Event details will indicate the course lengths and difficulties.

Unlike CATI and Club events where orienteers can register on the day, most Ranking and National events will require pre-entry, sometimes weeks or months before the event. It is therefore best to check entry details with the organizers well in advance.

National Championships and World Ranking events have higher status still and will inevitably require pre-entry. Entry to some courses will also be based on a competitor's national or international ranking.

The World Championships (to be held annually from 2003), the Junior World Championships (held annually) and World Cup (spread over a number of events held annually) are closed events. Competitors must apply for entry through their national federations. However, the World Masters Orienteering Championship (held annually) is an open event, which every orienteer over 35 is welcome to participate in.

NATIONAL EVENTS RUN COURSES ACCORDING TO IOF AGE GROUP CATEGORIES AND GENERALLY REQUIRE PRE-ENTRY.

Types of events

Foot orienteering is one of the four orienteering disciplines recognized by the International Orienteering Federation (IOF). The following forms of orienteering all fall into the broader category of foot orienteering and are practiced around the world:

Cross-country orienteering

Traditional or cross-country orienteering is the format used in all major events around the world including the World Championships. Cross-country orienteering involves navigating around a series of checkpoints in a given order. Competitors start at intervals (between 1—4 minutes apart) and the time taken to visit all the controls is recorded. The competitor who completes the course in the fastest time is the winner.

Courses can vary in length from a few hundred meters to 12—15km (7—10 miles) or more. The number of checkpoints will also vary from a few (usually not less than six) up to 30. The controls must be visited in a given order and competitors are disqualified if they visit them out of sequence or fail to visit a control altogether.

From its original concept, cross-country orienteering has developed into five distinct forms:

CROSS-COUNTRY ORIENTEERING COURSES IN EUROPE ARE GENERALLY SET IN — BUT NOT RESTRICTED TO — FOREST AREAS.

Long distance orienteering

Originally called classic distance orienteering, these were the first events included in the World Championships. For Open Men, the course distances range from 10–15km (6–9 miles), depending on the type of terrain, runnability and climbing to be done. Courses for the Open Women category will be 8–12km (5–8 miles), again depending on the physical nature of the course.

The winning times on such courses are generally 80–90 minutes for the Open Men category and 60–70 minutes for the Open Women category. Other age groups have correspondingly shorter winning times.

Middle distance orienteering

Middle distance orienteering (with winning times of between 30–35 minutes) was previously known as short distance orienteering. This category was first included in the World Championships in the Czech Republic in 1991.

Due to the short nature of the courses, competitors are running flat-out most of the time. Even a short course will include a lot of controls with distances between them averaging around 300m (1000ft). While it is possible to recover from minor mistakes in a long distance race, in a middle distance race, seconds are vital.

Sprint orienteering

Sprint orienteering courses are even shorter (and faster) than the short distance events described above. This particular format was developed in an attempt to increase the spectator value of orienteering events. With classic distance orienteering and, to a large extent, with short distance orienteering, the competitors are out of sight for all but the final few hundred meters of the course. Even with a spectator control, the spectator sees very little of the actual competition.

Sprint orienteering, developed as Park Orienteering by the Park World Tour (PWT) in the late 1990s, was an attempt to change previous parameters and allow spectators to be an intimate part of the race. These competitions are usually run through a mixture of park and town areas, and spectators are encouraged to watch competitors all around the course.

Speed is extremely important and while the courses may not offer the technical difficulty of traditional courses, competitors still need to navigate at top speed with seconds being vital. In this way the PWT has managed to take orienteering to countries where the sport is still underdeveloped.

The concept finally gained global acceptance with the inclusion of a sprint event in the 2001 World Championships in Finland.

SPRINT OR PARK ORIENTEERING EVENTS, FOR SELECTED INTERNATIONAL-STANDARD COMPETITORS ONLY, CAN TAKE YOU THROUGH RATHER UNUSUAL TERRAIN.

LONG DISTANCE ORIENTEERING AND MOUNTAIN MARATHONS ARE THE MOST PHYSICALLY DEMANDING FORMATS OF FOOT ORIENTEERING.

Ultra distance orienteering

Ultra distance events often take place on more than one map, necessitating a map exchange point somewhere on the course.

Longer distance does not necessarily mean a greater number of controls and there is scope for the planner to include long legs (2—3km; 1—2miles) of running and navigation between controls. Winning times in ultra distance orienteering events are generally greater than two hours.

Mountain marathons

Mountain marathons are extremely long in both distance and duration. As the name suggests, these events often take place in mountainous terrain and orienteers need to be extremely fit to compete.

Competitors normally compete in pairs and are required to carry enough equipment (food, clothing, tent, sleeping bag) to enable them to survive for the duration of the event, which usually includes an overnight camp.

Score orienteering

In score orienteering a number of controls are placed in a determined area and competitors have a certain amount of time, e.g. one hour, to 'score' as many points as possible. The controls furthest away from the start/finish earn higher points than those closer by.

Score orienteering is useful when a large number of competitors have to be accommodated in a small area or in a short space of time. The nature of the competition means that following is less likely. It also tests the orienteer's ability to estimate the distance that he or she can cover in the time allowed. High penalties are awarded for overrunning — it is therefore generally a good idea to return to the finish within the time allowed!

The score orienteering format is sometimes used in mountain marathons and also forms the basis for the sport of rogaining (*see* p74).

Relay orienteering

Whereas most orienteering events are races for the individual, relay events can also be held. In the most common type of orienteering relay, three or more competitors form a team and run a cross-country type course, one after the other, similar to an athletics relay.

The first leg runners usually start together as a group, but the course plan soon separates them. Each team member runs along a course set on a parallel line to the other competitors. The separate courses then meet up at a common control, only to branch out again on the next leg. All the courses converge on the same finish line in the end.

The second and third leg runners will start at the next course down from the previous runner, thus when all the team members have completed their respective courses, each team will have completed the same course overall.

Controls in relays are often placed very close to one another and competitors must ensure that they visit the correct control in the correct order by carefully checking the control code (generally a 3-digit number displayed on the control marker). Many a team has been disqualified in a relay for incorrect punching.

WITH CONTROLS PLACED QUITE CLOSE TOGETHER AND MANY MORE COMPETITORS ON THE COURSE, RELAY ORIENTEERING DEMANDS CONCENTRATION.

NIGHT ORIENTEERING IS PERHAPS THE MOST EXTREME OF ALL DISCIPLINES — FINDING YOUR WAY IN THE DARK HAS TO BE THE GREATEST CHALLENGE.

Night orienteering

All forms of orienteering described previously can be run at night. When the idea of night orienteering first developed, experiments were carried out with lit controls. However, the logisitics of having all the controls equally visible for the duration of the competition were difficult to overcome and most night events now use the standard orienteering control.

The only additional aid that the night orienteer is allowed is a torch or headlamp. A powerful double halogen headlamp, which affords visibility of several hundred meters under the right conditions, is obviously a major asset. Most night orienteers settle for a headlamp or powerful torch but it is always advisable to have a spare set of batteries. If your light fails then your night race is over and you still have to find your way back to the finish.

Orienteering at night can be extremely tricky since the competitor cannot see long distances and many features become more difficult to identify. It is critical that you keep in constant touch with the map and always know where you are. Relocating in the dark is much more difficult than during the day so caution is the keyword.

Other IOF disciplines

Ski orienteering

Orienteering is such a popular sport in the Nordic countries that it was only a matter of time before it was combined with the other popular Nordic sport, skiing. The result was ski orienteering, which is a fully-fledged discipline within the IOF.

Competitions are held regularly during winter and are based on similar concepts to foot orienteering, i.e. competitors must visit a series of checkpoints in a given order using a map and compass. However, ski orienteering takes place on a track network in an area where the competitor is faced with complex route choices including the estimation of height differences.

Maps for ski orienteering are based on the specifications for foot orienteering maps. However, they need to emphasize features to enable the skier to read the map at high speed — as a result, ski orienteering maps tend to omit a large part of the detail in the 'free' terrain and exaggerate the track network. They also simplify the presentation of the shape of the ground. Ski orienteering maps also make use of special symbols which indicate the quality and width of the tracks that the skier relies on. Maps often need to be updated shortly before an event in order to indicate the current state of the tracks in an area. The symbols used to update the map are printed onto the existing map in green.

As well as having a good pair of skis and appropriate clothing, the ski orienteer will need a map board which hangs around his neck leaving his hands free to ski. Ordinary control markers (as used in foot orienteering) and three different punching systems (manual, EMIT and SPORTident) are used in ski orienteering. Control descriptions are not used at all as all controls are situated on tracks.

Some of the major types of foot orienteering events (sprint, short distance, long distance and relay) are organized as ski orienteering events and World Championships and World Cups are also held in this discipline.

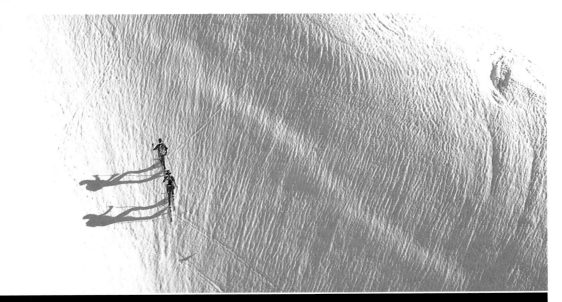

above OF THE FOUR ORIENTEERING DISCIPLINES, SKI ORIENTEERING HAS THE BEST CHANCE OF BEING INCLUDED IN THE OLYMPICS.

opposite WINTER ADVENTURE RACES IN THE NORDIC COUNTRIES HAVE BEEN KNOWN TO INCLUDE ASPECTS OF SKI ORIENTEERING, TAKEN TO EXTREMES.

Mountain bike orienteering

Mountain bike orienteering is the newest of the four IOF disciplines. It was developed in Europe during the 1990s and the first mountain bike World Championships were held in France in 2002.

Mountain bike orienteering is similar to ski orienteering in that competitors must navigate the track and path network in a given area in order to visit the controls. Competitors are not allowed to cycle freely through the terrain and the maps used for mountain bike orienteering must reflect this.

Maps must also be legible at high speed and as such, much of the detail found on foot orienteering maps is omitted. Mountain bike orienteering maps vary in scale from 1:10,000 to 1:30,000, the latter being used for longer distance races. Special attention is paid to the classification of tracks and paths on such maps and these are marked in black.

Similarly to ski orienteering, the map has to be mounted on a board which in this instance is attached to the handlebars of the bike. The board must be able to swivel so that the map can be correctly oriented at all times. This leaves both hands free to control the bike.

As with other bicycle sports, safety is an important consideration and the wearing of a helmet is a requirement in all mountain bike orienteering events.

above THE COURSE MAP IS MOUNTED ON A BOARD, WHICH IS ATTACHED TO THE HANDLEBARS OF THE MOUNTAIN BIKE.

opposite MOUNTAIN BIKE ORIENTEERING IS THE MOST RECENT INCLUSION IN THE SPORT, BUT ITS POPULARITY IS GROWING RAPIDLY.

Trail orienteering

Although most orienteering events cater for all abilities, traditional orienteering used to be practiced only by able-bodied people. Various attempts to widen the sport to include disabled participants were made in the 1980s. Trail orienteering was the result of these efforts and, confined to trails in the competition area, it allows disabled people the chance to compete as equals against able-bodied people in a variation of the sport.

The trail orienteer also uses a map and compass but instead of having to locate the controls in the terrain, they are visible from viewing points at certain places along the route. However, at each viewing point two or more controls are visible and the competitor must decide which one is the control marked on the map using the control description sheet and his or her map reading skills accordingly.

Normal foot orienteering maps can be used but maps at 1:5000 are generally preferred due to the length of the courses and the degree of detail that is required.

A slightly different control card is used, with a number of boxes (marked A, B, C, etc.) for each control. Controls are always marked from A, which is the leftmost one as viewed by the competitor. Having made a choice the competitor punches in the appropriate box on the control card, corresponding to the letter of the selected control.

Courses are graded according to the level of map-reading ability required and not according to age, gender or type of disability.

There is generally no time pressure on competitors — the skill is to select the correct control marker and competitors can take as long as they need to make their decision.

At the highest level, trail orienteering is practiced competitively and it is necessary to have one or more timed controls at which the time taken in selecting the correct control is measured. While this time is used in case of a tie on the number of correct controls identified, there is still no time limit on the completion of the course.

The World Cup and European Championships for trail orienteering, open only to disabled competitors, were held in conjunction with the 2001 Foot Orienteering World Championships in Tampere, Finland.

TRAIL ORIENTEERING HAS OPENED THE SPORT TO DISABLED PEOPLE.

Other types of orienteering

As well as the official forms of orienteering discussed in this chapter, there are other varieties including horseback, canoeing and even underwater orienteering.

These tend to be practiced by specialists in the sport concerned or are included as a feature in multi-disciplinary sport events. The navigational principles involved remain the same.

THE BASIC PRINCIPLES OF NAVIGATION REMAIN THE SAME WHEREVER YOU DECIDE TO SET AN ORIENTEERING COURSE — EVEN UNDERWATER!

The Scope of 'O'

Various forms of orienteering, not just the four IOF disciplines, have been included in multi-discipline sporting events. The basic navigation techniques, whether on foot, in a boat, on a bicycle or in a vehicle remain the same, and the number of people wanting to learn these techniques is likely to increase.

Endurance events such as Raid Gauloises and Camel Trophy have incorporated navigation in their challenges for many years. More recently, Adventure Racing and Eco Challenges — in which teams, usually consisting of four people, have to travel distances of between 60–600km (40–400 miles) by canoe, boat, swimming, bicycle or on foot — have become very popular. Many of the legs also include navigation, and the techniques described earlier in this book are still relevant, irrespective of the discipline.

Rogaining

The sport of rogaining, despite the similarities to orienteering, does not fall under the control of the IOF. Practiced mainly in Australia and the USA, rogaining is essentially a long duration foot score orienteering event.

Competitors compete in teams of two to five people over either 12, or more frequently, 24 hours. In that time they have to visit as many checkpoints set out in a determined area as possible. Teams can return to the competition center at any time to eat, rest or sleep. Competitors must decide on which checkpoints to visit within the allowed time and how long they will rest/sleep, if at all.

Events cater for all levels of ability and fitness. While some competitors will walk leisurely around the area, those in the top teams may cover over 100km (60 miles) in a 24-hour event.

Unlike orienteering, where the control points are either pre-marked on the map or copied from a master map, rogaining competitors must calculate the sites of the controls from given coordinates. To this end, the map is divided into squares using a numbered grid system. The grid reference of a location is usually given as two three-digit numbers. The first three digits represent the east—west location and the second three digits represent the north—south location. The first two digits are the number of the line immediately to the west/left of the location and the third is the number of tenths from this line to the location. Similarly, the fourth and fifth digits are the number of the line to the south or below the location with the sixth digit being the number of tenths from this line to the location.

above ROGAINING TEAMS CONSIST OF TWO TO FIVE MEMBERS WHO COMPETE IN A DETERMINED AREA. COMPETITONS ARE GENERALLY HELD OVER A 24-HOUR PERIOD.

opposite ENDURACE EVENTS SUCH AS ADVENTURE RACING DRAW ON A NUMBER OF SKILLS — COMPETITORS MUST BE EQUALLY PROFICIENT ON FOOT, SWIMMING, ON A BIKE OR IN A BOAT.

As with many other sports, orienteering is changing as new technology becomes available. Electronic punching is now the norm at all major events. Not only does this simplify the timing and results but split times are available for the competitors.

Software

Several different computer software programs are available to assist with event organization from entries, through course planning, to results. Special programs are also available for the generation of IOF control description sheets.

Orienteering simulation software has even been developed. While nowhere near as good as actually running through the forest, armchair orienteers can sit at a computer and have their navigation abilities tested to the full.

ENDURACE EVENTS SUCH AS THE CAMEL TROPHY MAKE USE OF GLOBAL POSITIONING SATELLITE (GPS) READERS.

Mapping

Map drawing used to be a tedious chore as the symbols for each color had to be drawn manually on a separate sheet of film to allow the map to be printed in five colors. These days computer-aided drafting (CAD) programs specifically developed for orienteering maps have made life much easier.

Improved printing technology has also helped. The original method of litho printing is still used where large quantities of maps and high quality reproduction are required. However, areas tend to change over time and printed maps soon become out of date. With development in computers, other forms of printing can now be used. Small quantities of maps can be printed using inkjet or color laser printers. The number of maps required for an event are printed, changes can easily be made and the map reprinted before the area is used again.

Navigation

Officially, the only navigation aids allowed in the sport of orienteering are a compass and the map provided by the organizers. However, several endurance events and other related disciplines are making increasing use of Global Positioning Satellite (GPS) readers.

In orienteering proper, the biggest use of GPS is currently seen in mapping, where such a system allows plot data to be transferred from the ground to a computer with ease. Such developments are still in their early stages, but this technique is likely to make mapping easier in future.

In other forms of competition which include navigation, such as adventure racing, GPS readers are often used. The GPS works by using a number of satellites to pinpoint the exact position of the sensing device. The results can be incredibly accurate and will show your position to within 50m (55yd). Originally developed for military use, systems have now become affordable and are used more commonly.

Spectator appeal

Orienteering has traditionally not been a spectator-friendly sport. Competitors disappear into a forest, only to emerge 60–90 minutes later. Despite improvements in technology, what goes on out in the forest remains much of a mystery to spectators until after the event.

Radical changes in terms of event format and the development of existing technology may well change the spectator appeal of the sport in the future. An exciting development has been the introduction of tracking devices which can be worn by competitors, enabling their position to be shown on a large electronic map situated at the finish area.

Such a system was used for the first time in a major competition at the 2001 World Championships in Tampere, Finland. The 200g (7oz) device carried by each competitor allowed real-time tracking of the top contenders through the forest, with spectators able to observe their mistakes and successes as they moved from control to control.

The possibilities of such a tracking system for large orienteering events are currently being explored and a development in this field could add a new dimension for spectators in future.

The IOF is also experimenting with the possibility of allowing spectators to observe competitors on selected parts of the course. However, this has to be achieved without removing the essence of orienteering, which requires a competitor to navigate through unknown terrain. The delicate balance has not yet been finalized.

THE DEVELOPMENT OF NEW TECHNOLOGIES COULD MEAN THAT IN THE FUTURE SPECTATOR INVOLVEMENT WILL NOT BE LIMITED TO THE FINISH LINE.

FOOT ORIENTEERING EVENTS ARE NOT ALWAYS HELD IN 'GREEN' SURROUNDINGS — THIS PARK COURSE SET IN GRAZ, AUSTRIA, SAW ORIENTEERS BATTLING NOT ONLY OTHER COMPETITORS, BUT PEDESTRIANS AS WELL!

Orienteering — the thought sport

So what makes orienteering so different to other sports? What exactly is it that attracts people to this combination of physical and mental exercise? With a constantly increasing number of orienteering clubs and associations springing up around the world, it is evident that the sport continues to grow in popularity. Why? Four well-known orienteers share a few of their own experiences along with their enthusiasm for orienteering.

Carsten Jørgensen, Danish international orienteer and past European cross-country champion:

'I started orienteering at the age of 10 and became hooked straight away. I loved the thrill of adventure that I got running through the forest looking for the controls. I loved competing in an individual sport. But most of all I loved bending the rules and not sticking to the tracks!

Today, I'm still hooked. I still can't get enough of the adventure. Nothing compares to running through a forest, knowing exactly where to go because you've trained hard and you have a good map in your hands. Now I get to travel all over the world, competing at an international level, and making friends with others who share my fascination with the sport and the outdoors.'

Peo Bengtsson, the Swedish orienteering pioneer, has participated in events in 58 countries and introduced the sport to a good number of them:

'In 1949, when I was 15, I ran my first training orienteering competition. As I continued to take part in competitions, I became increasingly interested and made better results. During the summers of 1961 and 1963, I organized tours from the south of Sweden to competitions in Denmark, Germany and Switzerland. Later, as a member of O-Ringen — the club for Swedish national team runners — I actively pursued their goal of developing orienteering into a more international sport. We were successful. Today orienteering is practiced on all continents and I have organized tours to countries all over the world.'

Jörgen Mårtensson, Swedish international orienteer and past World Orienteering champion:

'In my days as an elite-orienteer, competitions offered me the opportunity to master my own body on both a physical and a mental level. You combine all your skills in order to make fast decisions under immense pressure — this does not just make you a good athlete, it also rounds off other aspects of your life and helps you to become a better student, organizer or leader.

Orienteering is an extremely tough sport and to become an elite runner you must put in long hours of training every day. The adventure, however, makes it all worth while — and you can still enjoy this thrill even if you don't compete at a professional level.

Orienteering is spreading rapidly, and has begun to develop into two distinct formats: forest orienteering and park orienteering. The sport is currently practiced in 58 countries around the world and is growing each year. The mecca of orienteering, however, remains Scandinavia where orienteering started just over 100 years ago. The largest event in the world is the annual Swedish 5-day O-Rringen which attracts up to 25,000 competitors from all over the world.'

Martin Terry, one of South Africa's top orienteers and a recognized force in the international arena, moved to Sweden to be closer to the sport:

'Orienteering takes me to some of the most beautiful places in the world. I can still remember one of the first times I went to Swaziland, back when orienteering first started in South Africa. It was cold and raining but what really stuck in my mind were the smells of the wet forest. Today, when I am out running in the forest, I'll get a whiff of something that brings back a memory of some other forest.

Orienteering is a sport of multiple talents that must all be brought together in competition. The challenge of having to make a decision fast and to follow it all the way through is hard. Orienteering is a new challenge every time: new forests and different types of terrain, but always that familiar rush of adrenaline.

Moving to Sweden has made a dream come true. A sticker that I had when I was a child said: 'Orienteering, a way of living'. I never really understood it until I came here and saw how hooked people are on the sport and how their lives revolve around it. Now I know exactly what that sticker meant and I live by it. Orienteering is truly a way of life, so live it!'

Orienteering Worldwide

now that you're hooked, you will no doubt want to regularly attend events where you can practice your newfound skills. The major orienteering federations can offer valuable advice and information on upcoming events in your area.

Information on orienteering is also freely available on the Internet and many excellent sites can be visited. These include details of forthcoming events, event results, details of local clubs, rules, available software, maps and the latest developments in the sport.

Worldwide orienteering federations

INTERNATIONAL ORIENTEERING FEDERATION (IOF)
- Radiokatu 20, FI–00093 SLU
- Tel: +358 (9) 3481 3112
- Fax: +358 (9) 3481 3113
- E-mail: iof@orienteering.org
- Website: www.orienteering.org

AUSTRALIA
- Orienteering Federation of Australia
- PO Box 740, Glebe, NSW 2037
- Tel: +61 (29) 660 2067
- Fax: +61 (29) 660 2067
- E-mail: Orienteering@dsr.nsw.gov.au
- Website: www.sportnet.com.au/orienteering

AUSTRIA
- Österreichischer Fachverband für OL
- Prinz Eugenstraße 12
- AT–1040 Wien, Austria
- Tel: +43 (1) 505 0393
- Fax: +43 (1) 505 0393
- E-mail: office@oefol.at
- Website: www.oefol.at

BELGIUM
- Belgische Vereiniging voor Orienteringssporten
- c/o Jan Herremans, Meerhoef 12, B–3971 Leopoldsburg
- Tel/Fax: +32 (11) 343 301
- E-mail: Bart.Herremans@ping.be
- Website: www.abso-bvos.org

BULGARIA
- Bulgarian Orienteering Federation
- Box 427, Bul Vassil Levski 75, BG–1000, Sofia
- Tel: +359 (2) 930 0613
- Fax: +359 (2) 987 4427
- E-mail: bgof@mail.prosoft.bg

CANADA
- The Canadian Orienteering Federation
- Box 62052, Convent Glen PO, Orleans, Ontario K1C 7H8
- Tel: +1 (613) 830 1147
- Fax: +1 (613) 830 0456
- E-mail: ckirk@rtm.cdnsport.ca
- Website: www.orienteering.ca

CHINA
- Orienteering Association of China
- A14 Tiantan Dingli Zhongqu, CN–100061, Beijing
- Tel: +86 (10) 6702 0165
- Fax: +86 (10) 6701 6974
- E-mail: crsa@public.bta.net.cn

opposite ORIENTEERING EVENTS – CROSS-COUNTRY, NIGHT, SPRINT, LONG DISTANCE EVENTS OR EVEN MOUNTAIN MARATHONS – CAN BE FOUND ALL OVER THE WORLD. ALL YOU NEED TO DO IS CONTACT YOUR NEAREST ASSOCIATION FOR DETAILS ON EVENTS IN YOUR AREA.

CZECH REPUBLIC

- Cesky svaz orientacniho behu
- POB 40, Mezi stadiony, CZ–16017 Praha 6 – Strahov
- Tel: +420 (2) 2051 3295
- Fax: +420 (2) 2051 3295
- E-mail: csob@cstv.cz
- Website: www-ob.fsv.cvut.cz

DENMARK

- Dansk Orienterings-Forbund
- Idraettens Hus, Bröndby Stadion 20, DK–2605, Bröndby
- Tel: +45 (43) 457 730
- Fax: +45 (43) 457 790
- E-mail: dof@dif.dk
- Website: www.dk.orienteering.org

FINLAND

- Suomen Suunnistusliitto, Radiokatu 20, FI–00093 SLU
- Tel: +358 (9) 3481 2453
- Fax: +358 (9) 3481 2433
- E-mail: info@ssl.fi
- Website: www.ssl.fi

FRANCE

- Fédération Française de Course d'Orientation
- BP 220, FR–75967, Paris Cedex 20
- Tel: +33 (1) 47 91 11 91
- Fax: +33 (1) 47 97 90 29
- E-mail: ffco@compuserve.com
- Website: www.ffco.asso.fr

GREAT BRITAIN

- British Orienteering Federation
- Riversdale, Dale Road North, Darley Dale Matlock Derbyshire DE4 2HX
- Tel: +44 (1629) 734 042
- Fax: +44 (1629) 733 769
- E-mail: bof@bof.cix.co.uk
- Website: www.britishorienteering.org.uk

GERMANY

- Deutscher Turner Bund Abteilung Sport Orientierungslauf
- Otto-Fleck-Schneisse 8, DE–60528, Frankfurt-am-Main
- Tel: +49 (69) 6780 10
- Fax: +49 (69) 6780 1179
- E-mail: vorsitz@orientierungslauf.de
- Website: www.orientierungslauf.de

left FRANCE WAS ONE OF THE PIONEERS OF MOUNTAIN BIKE ORIENTEERING BUT MANY FOOT ORIENTEERING EVENTS ALSO TAKE PLACE HERE.

JAPAN WAS THE LOCATION OF THE WORLD GAMES IN 2001. THE WORLD FOOT ORIENTEERING CHAMPIONSHIPS WILL BE HELD HERE IN 2005.

HONG KONG

- Orienteering Association of Hong Kong
- Room 1014, Sports House, 1 Stadium Path
  So Kon Po, Causeway Bay
- Tel: +852 (2) 504 8111
- Fax: +852 (2) 577 5595
- E-mail: info@oahk.org.hk
- Website: www.oahk.org.hk

HUNGARY

- Magyar Tájékozódási Futó Szövetség
- Dózsa Gy. út 1–3, HU–1143 Budapest
- Tel: +36 (1) 2215878
- Fax: +36 (1) 2215878
- E-mail: mtfsz@mail.datanet.hu
- Website: lazarus.elte.hu/tajfutas/

IRELAND

- Irish Orienteering Association
- 86 Meadow Vale, Blackrock, Co. Dublin
- Tel: +353 (1) 450 9845
- E-mail: irishoa@tinet.ie
- Website: http://orienteering.ie

ISRAEL

- Israel Sport Orienteering Association
- POB 335, Hod Hasharon 45102
- Tel: +972 9 898 7970
- Fax: +972 9 894 6550
- E-mail: nivut@netvision.net.il
- Website: www.orienteering.org.il

ITALY

- Federazione Italiana Sport Orientamento
- Piazza San Pellico 5, IT–38100 Trento
- Tel: +39 (0461) 231 380
- Fax: +39 (0461) 236 424
- E-mail: fiso@technotn.it
- Website: www.fiso.it

JAPAN

- Nihon Orienteering Kyokai
- Kastanie Shiba Building 2F, 3–28–2 Shiba
  Minato-ku JP–105 Tokyo
- Tel: +81 (3) 5476 5657
- Fax: +81 (3) 5476 5658
- E-mail: orienteering@japan-sports.or.jp

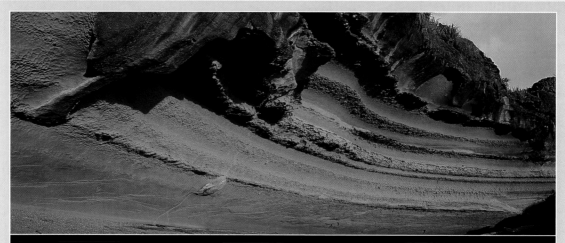

AUSTRALIA IS THE LARGEST AND STRONGEST ORIENTEERING COUNTRY OUTSIDE EUROPE. IT WAS THE VENUE FOR THE WORLD ORIENTEERING CHAMPIONSHIPS IN 1985 AND WILL HOST THE WORLD MASTERS ORIENTEERING CHAMPIONSHIPS IN OCTOBER 2002.

NETHERLANDS

- Nederlandse Orienteringsloop Bond
- Ooievaardspad 7, 3403 AM, Ijsselstein
- Tel: +31 (30) 688 8759
- E-mail: kraaikam@hetnet.nl
- Website: www.xs4all.nl/~klaver80/NOLB

NORWAY

- Norges Orienteringsforbund
- Serviceboks 1, Ullevål Stadion, NO−0840 Oslo
- Tel: +47 (2) 1029 000
- Fax: +47 (2) 1029 511
- E-mail: nof@orientering.no
- Website: orientering.no

NEW ZEALAND

- New Zealand Orienteering Federation
- 171A Fitfield Terrace, Opawa, Christchurch 2
- Tel: +64 (3) 337 2275
- Fax: +64 (3) 337 2275
- E-mail: nzof@nzorienteering.com
- Website: www.nzorienteering.com

POLAND

- Polski Zwiazek Biegu na Orientacje
- Ul. Wilcza 38A, PL00679 Warszawa
- Tel: +48 (22) 629 5004
- Fax: +48 (22) 629 5004
- E-mail: orienteering@orienteering.org.pl
- Website: www.orienteering.org.pl

PORTUGAL

- Federação Portuguesa de Orientação
- Apartado 2, PT−2644−909 Mafra
- Tel: +351 (261) 819 171
- Fax: +351 (261) 819 173
- E-mail: fpo@mail.telepac.pt
- Website: www.fpo.pt

ROMANIA

- Federatia Româna de Orientare
- B-dul Basarabia 37−39, Sector 2, RO−73403 Bucharesti
- Tel: +40 (1) 324 5375
- Fax: +40 (1) 250 2569
- E-mail: romofed@yahoo.com
- Website: www.geocities.com/romofed

RUSSIA

- Orienteering Federation of Russia
- Box 57, Moscow, 123060
- Tel: +7 (095) 196 9089
- Fax: +7 (095) 196 7155
- E-mail: ntorient@cityline.ru
- Website: www.welcome.to/rus_orienteering

SLOVENIA

- Orientacijska Zveza Slovenije
- Legatova 6a, SI–1000 Ljubljana
- Tel: +386 (61) 125 0676 (Dusan Petrovic)
- Fax: +386 (61) 125 0677 (Dusan Petrovic)
- E-mail: dusan.petrovic@geod-is.si
- Website: www.orientacijska-zveza.si

SOUTH AFRICA

- South African Orienteering Federation
- PO Box 8968, Cinda Park, ZA–1463, Gauteng
- Tel: +27 (11) 360 3046
- Fax: +27 (11) 360 3266
- E-mail: ianbratt@global.co.za
- Website: www.orienteering.org.za

SPAIN

- Agrupación Española de Clubes de Orientación
- SG Jesús de Miguel Rey, Gran Via, 66–8, Of. 16
  ES–28013 Madrid
- Tel: +34 (1) 542 0880
- Fax: +34 (1) 542 0880
- E-mail: aeco1@arrakis.es

SWEDEN

- Svenska Orienteringsförbundet
- Idrottens Hus, SE–123 87 Farsta
- Tel: +46 (8) 605 6000
- Fax: +46 (8) 605 6360
- E-mail: info@orientering.se
- Website: www.orientering.se

SWITZERLAND

- Schweizerischer Orientierungslauf-Verband
- Langweidstrasse 2, CH–8620 Wetzikon
- Tel: +41 (1) 932 5080
- Fax: +41 (1) 932 5084
- E-mail: solv@active.ch
- Website: www.solv.ch

USA

- United States Orienteering Federation
- PO Box 1444, Forest Park, GA 30298
- Tel: +1 (404) 363 2110
- Fax: +1 (404) 363 2110
- E-mail: 75454.121@compuserve.com
- Website: www.us.orienteering.org/

THE USA WAS THE VENUE FOR THE 1993 WORLD (FOOT) ORIENTEERING CHAMPIONSHIPS. EVENTS ARE HELD REGULARLY IN MANY PARTS OF THE COUNTRY.

IOF international control description symbols

The International Orienteering Federation (IOF) has produced a list of symbol descriptions for international usage so that orienteers from all countries can understand control descriptions without ambiguity or translation.

A control description is used to provide an exact specification of the control feature and the location of the marker in relation to this feature. A control description sheet contains this information for the entire course.

How to read a control description sheet

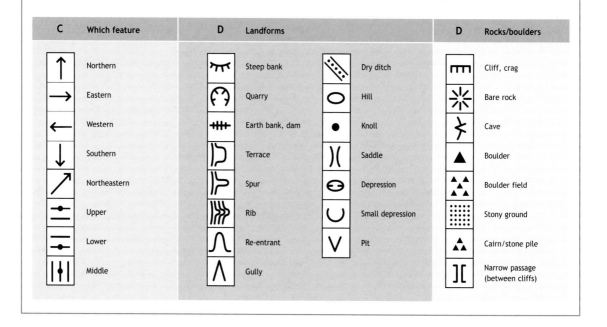

Class	Climbing in meters	Course length in metres

A   B   C   D   E   F   G   H

7 | 3 2 | ↓ | ▲ | ◇ | 2× | Ȯ | ✚

The most important items lie to the right of the thicker lines

This indicates a tape route to the finish (230m)

This indicates navigate (no tapes) to the finish (160m)

Each control is described in a separate column, labelled A–H, as follows:

A ⸢7⸥ **Control Number**
The control number in sequence around the course.

B ⸢3 2⸥ **Control Code**
The identifying number on the control marker.

C ⸢↓⸥ **Which feature**
Where there is more than one similar feature within a circle, in this case the southern.

D ⸢▲⸥ **Control feature**
Normally the map symbol, in this instance a boulder.

E ⸢◇⸥ **Further information**
More information on the feature, in this case open land/field.

F ⸢2×3⸥ **Size of the feature**
Dimensions in metres.

G ⸢Ȯ⸥ **Position of the marker**
Where on/in the control feature the marker is located, in this case the north side.

H ⸢✚⸥ **Other important info**
In this instance, refreshments.

And so the description reads: Control 7 (32), the southern-most boulder in an open field, 2x3m, on the north side of the boulder, first aid available.

C	Which feature	D	Landforms			D	Rocks/boulders
↑	Northern	🝏	Steep bank	⸭	Dry ditch	⊞	Cliff, crag
→	Eastern	⌒	Quarry	◯	Hill	✳	Bare rock
←	Western	⪫	Earth bank, dam	●	Knoll	人	Cave
↓	Southern	⏦	Terrace	)(	Saddle	▲	Boulder
↗	Northeastern	⏦	Spur	⊝	Depression	⸪	Boulder field
⊸	Upper	⫴	Rib	∪	Small depression	⁘	Stony ground
⊸	Lower	⋀	Re-entrant	∨	Pit	⛰	Cairn/stone pile
⫴	Middle	⋀	Gully			)(	Narrow passage (between cliffs)

D	Water/marsh	D	Vegetation	D	Man-made features	D	Additional features
	Lake		Open land, field		Road		Shooting platform
	Pond		Semi-open land		Path		Fodder rack
	Waterhole		Forest corner		Narrow ride		Rock pillar
	Stream		Clearing		Wall		Single tree
	Ditch		Thicket		Fence		Salt lick
	Marsh		Felled area		Footbridge		Root stock
	Small marsh		Vegetation boundary		Building		Boundary stone
	Firm ground		Copse		Ruin		Charcoal burning ground
	Well		Hedge		Tower		Anthill
	Spring		Linear thicket		Powerline		Broken ground, fox-earth
	Narrow marsh				Powerline pylon/pole		Special items the definitions of which must be supplied in advance
	Seasonal watercourse						

E	Appearance	F	Dimensions	G	Location		
	Shallow	5.5	Height in metres		North side		At the foot
	Deep	7x	Size in metres		Northwest edge		Southwest end
	Overgrown	1. 2.	Height of object on a slope		East corner (inside)		Between
	Open	1. 2.	Height of two objects in Column D		Southwest corner		Bend
	Rocky				Southern tip		
	Marshy				Western part	G	Other relevant info
	Sandy				Upper part (head)		Refreshments
	Coniferous				Lower part (foot)		Radio control
	Deciduous				On top of ...		Control check
	Ruined or collapsed				Southern foot		First aid

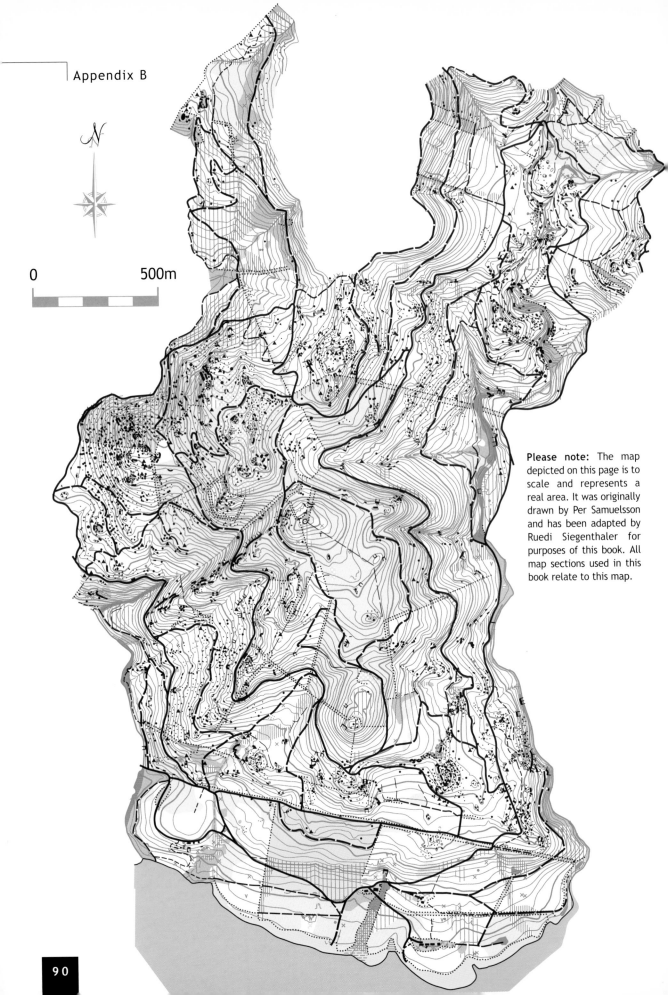

0　　　　　　500m

Please note: The map depicted on this page is to scale and represents a real area. It was originally drawn by Per Samuelsson and has been adapted by Ruedi Siegenthaler for purposes of this book. All map sections used in this book relate to this map.

Map symbols

Landforms

- contour
- index contour
- form line
- earthbank
- earth wall
- small earth wall
- erosion gully
- small erosion gully
- knoll
- small knoll
- depression
- small depression
- pit
- broken ground
- special landform feature
- impassable cliff
- rock pillar/cliff
- passable cliff
- rocky pit
- cave
- boulder
- large boulder
- boulder field
- boulder cluster
- stony ground
- open sandy ground
- bare rock

Water features

- lake
- pond
- waterhole
- uncrossable river
- crossable watercourse
- crossable watercourse & foot bridge
- minor water channel
- narrow marsh
- uncrossable marsh
- marsh
- indistinct marsh
- well
- spring/stream
- special water feature

Vegetation

- open land
- open land & scattered trees
- rough open land
- rough open land & scattered trees
- orchard
- vineyard
- cultivated land
- forest: easy running
- forest: slow running
- undergrowth: slow running
- forest: difficult to run
- undergrowth: difficult to run
- vegetation: impassable
- forest: runnable in one direction
- distinct vegetation boundary
- indistinct vegetation boundary
- special vegetation feature

Man-made features

- motorway
- major road
- minor road
- road
- vehicle track
- footpath
- small footpath
- less distinct small footpath
- railway
- power line
- major power line
- stone wall
- ruined wall
- high stone wall
- fence
- ruined fence
- high fence
- crossing point
- narrow ride
- narrow ride, open
- wide ride
- tunnel
- ruin
- building
- settlement
- permanently out of bounds
- parking area
- sports track
- firing range
- cemetery
- grave
- crossable pipeline
- uncrossable pipeline
- high tower
- small tower
- cairn
- fodder
- special man-made feature

IOF age group categories

Category M (men)	Age	Category W (women)
M10	10 and under	W10
M12	11/12	W12
M14	13/14	W14
M16	15/16	W16
M18	17/18	W18
M20	19/20	W20
M21 (open)	Any age from 21—35	W21 (open)
M35	35—39	W35
M40	40—44	W40
M45	45—49	W45
M50	50—54	W50
M55	55—59	W55
M60	60—64	W60
M65	65—69	W65
M70	70—74	W70
M75	75—79	W75
M80	80—84	W80
M85	85 and older	W85

Competitors aged 20 and under belong to their respective class until the end of the calendar year in which they reach the given age. They are entitled to compete in older classes up to and including 21.

Competitors aged 20 and older belong to their respective class from the beginning of the calendar year in which they reach the given age. They may compete in younger classes down to and including 21.

In some countries the letters H (Herrar or Herren) and D (Damer or Damen) are used instead of M and W, respectively.

THERE ARE ORIENTEERING COURSES AVAILABLE FOR ALL AGE GROUPS, SET COMMENSURATE WITH THE PARTICPANTS' PHYSICAL ABILITY.

Glossary

Aiming off Deliberately running on a bearing to the left or right of the correct one so that when a line feature is encountered one knows which way to turn.

Attack point An obvious feature close to a control that is easier to find than the control itself. If the competitor finds the attack point he or she will find it much easier to proceed to the control.

Base plate The part of the compass which holds the compass housing.

Bearing The direction of travel as indicated by the compass.

Bramble bashers Long socks with reinforcements over the shins that provide some protection from vegetation. An alternative to gaiters.

Catching feature A large feature situated beyond the control used if the control is overshot. Also known as a collecting feature.

Collecting feature *see* catching feature.

Contour A line on the map joining places of equal height.

Contour interval The vertical distance between contours, which is typically 5m (15ft) for orienteering maps.

Control Checkpoints that the competitor must visit. A trapezoid-shaped flag (usually orange and white) marks the control, which usually has a punching device attached to it to mark the control card and thus verify the visit.

Control card A card on which punch marks are made at each control to enable organizers to determine if a competitor has visited all the controls.

Control code Letters (or numbers) on a marker which enable the participant to verify that it is the correct one.

Control description A description of the physical location or feature on which the control is situated. This can include the type of feature and its size, among others.

Control description sheet A list given to each participant which briefly describes each control feature in order. The list also gives the control code.

Course A sequence of control points marked on the map which are to be visited by the orienteer.

EMIT An electronic punching device making use of a credit card size 'card'. The card is placed into a recessed slot on the punching device located at each control.

Fartlek A method of running training where the speed and effort are varied within the same run.

Fight Extremely difficult terrain. Progress through such areas is very slow and competitors are usually advised to avoid if at all possible. Depicted as dark green on maps.

Fine navigation Involves using detailed features on the map to navigate into the control. Practiced when a competitor is close to a control and he or she slows down to take more care.

Foot orienteering Competitors participate on foot and no mechanical aids are permitted. Foot orienteering is one of the four official IOF disciplines.

Handrail A linear feature such as a fence or road that can be followed easily.

IOF International Orienteering Federation.

Kite Another name for a control.

Knoll A small hill.

Leg The section of a course between two controls.

Legend The key to all symbols on a map. Orienteering maps all over the world use standard symbols.

Line feature Any feature which extends over a fairly long distance, e.g. a fence, road or stream. Generally easier to find than a point feature.

Magnetic north The direction to which the red end of the compass needle points. The north lines on an orienteering map also point to magnetic north.

Map A two-dimensional depiction of the terrain. Orienteering maps are specifically drawn for the sport since they have to be highly detailed. Special symbols are used to depict various features. An international standard exists for orienteering maps so that maps are standardized worldwide.

Master map A map which has the course marked on it, located at the start. The competitor must use this map as reference and copy down the control locations onto his or her own (blank) map before setting off on the course.

Mountain bike orienteering Competitors participate on mountain bikes over similar terrain and using similar maps to foot orienteering. Courses tend to be correspondingly longer. Mountain bike orienteering is one of the four official IOF disciplines.

Needle punch A device for punching the competitor's control card. The needle pattern for each control is unique, allowing organizers to verify that the correct control was visited. Electronic punching devices, such as EMIT and SPORTident, are more advanced mechanisms that make use of a 'smart card'.

O Common abbreviated term for Orienteering, as in O-map, O-shoes, etc.

O-CAD A computer program widely used for drawing orienteering maps.

Pace counting The practice of measuring distance using your own (known) pace length.

Parallel error A navigational error. The competitor believes he is in one place, when he is actually at a similar feature some distance away.

Park orienteering A spectator-friendly type of orienteering which is run in a public park. Usually only one course is set, suitable for all abilities, with competitors starting at one-minute intervals.

Point feature A feature which does not have any appreciable length and is easy to miss if the competitor is slightly off bearing, e.g. a small building, a knoll, a boulder.

Pre-entry A competition where entries have to be submitted to the organizers prior to the event.

Pre-marked map A map on which the course is already marked. Standard at larger events, especially pre-entry events; competitors usually receive a pre-marked map as they start the course.

Pre-start The area into which competitors are called a few minutes before their start time.

Re-entrant A small valley or hollow in a hillside. On a map, the contour lines which describe a re-entrant point uphill.

Relocation Trying to find out where you are after you become disoriented. Usually achieved by heading in a known direction until an obvious feature is reached.

RICE Formula for treating injuries — Rest, Ice, Compression, Elevation.

Ride A gap in the trees or forest such as a fire-break.

Rough navigation Heading in a general direction without taking too much notice of the fine detail on the map. Generally carried out at the fastest speed a competitor can manage.

Route choice The art of choosing the best route on a particular leg.

Run Terrain which allows rapid progress. Usually marked with white (forests) or dark yellow (open) on maps.

Runnability The ease or speed at which a competitor is able to run through a given type of terrain. Forest terrain is marked with varying shades of green and open terrain with varying shades of yellow. Types of terrain, e.g. thick vegetation, rocks and marsh may reduce runnability.

Scale The distance on the ground represented by distance on the map. Normal orienteering maps are 1:10,000 (1cm on the map represents 100m on the ground) or 1:15,000 (1cm on the map represents 150m on the ground).

Setting the map Orientating the map so that it matches the ground.

Ski orienteering Competitors participate on skis over similar terrain and using similar maps to other orienteering disciplines. Courses are correspondingly longer. Ski orienteering is one of the four official IOF disciplines.

SPORTident An electronic punching device, cylindrical in shape and about 5cm (2in) in length. The device must be inserted into a hole at each control and an audible tone indicates that the device has registered the visit.

Stake control A control not marked with the usual kite but with a metal stake, painted red and white, with a punch fixed on top. These are used when kites would be too visible or are likely to be stolen.

String course A course for very young children marked by streamers or string.

Thumbing Holding the map folded with your thumb indicating your current location.

Trail orienteering Orienteering for disabled people. Trail orienteering is one of the four official IOF disciplines.

Vegetation The type of growth (trees, grass, bushes) that occurs in a particular area.

Vegetation boundary Where the vegetation changes from one type to another.

Visibility The distance that you can see through wooded terrain. Visibility may be good where runnability is poor.

Walk An area in which the competitor is likely to make slow progress. Usually indicated with pale green (forest) or pale yellow (open) on the map.

Index

Photographic credits

Publishers' acknowledgments: The publishers wish to thank Colin Dutkiewicz for his valuable input, Ruedi Siegenthaler for supplying maps that met our demanding specifications, Ali Kuosku from Silva for providing images of orienteering clothing, Pat Devine of Hi-tec South Africa for supplying the Adventure Racing image, Grant Buckley for the 3-D renditions of contours, Peter Palmer for allowing us to draw on his relocation panel, Carl Germishuys for his cartographic assistance, Kurt van Vreede and Mark Corbett for all their help during photoshoots and with the book in general.

All photographs by Nicholas Aldridge/New Holland Image Library with the exception of the following:

4–5	Keith Samuelson	64	Erik Borg
6–7	Jonathan Taylor	65	Peder Sundström
8	Jonathan Taylor	66	Jonathan Taylor
10	Keith Samuelson	67	Keith Samuelson
11	Peder Sundström	68	Peder Sundström
13	Peder Sundström	69	Peder Sundström
15a	Keith Samuelson	70	Kamil Arnost
19	Michael Brett	71	Jonathan Taylor
20	Gallo Images	72	Keith Samuelson
24	Holger Leue	73	Andy Belcher
28a	Gallo Images	74	Peder Sundström
38	Keith Samuelson	75	Hi-tec South Africa
42	Greg Sack	77	Compassport
46–47	SIL/Ryno Reyneke	78–79	Erik Borg
48a	SIL/Ryno Reyneke	80a	Keith Samuelson
48c	Erik Borg	80b	Keith Samuelson
49	Jonathan Taylor	81a	Keith Samuelson
52c	Keith Samuelson	81b	Glen Terry
54	Erik Borg	82	Peder Sundström
57	SPORTident/Diethard Kundisch	84	Caroline Jones
58	Jonathan Taylor	85	Tony Stone/Gallo Images
59	Keith Samuelson	86	Shaun Barnett
62	Keith Samuelson	87	Robert Harding Picture Library
63	Keith Samuelson	92	Jonathan Taylor

References and further reading

Bagness, Martin. (1995). *Outward Bound Orienteering Handbook*. London: Ward Lock.
McNeill, Carol. (1989). *Orienteering The Skills of the Game*. Marlborough: The Crowood Press.
Hogedal, Lasse. (1999). *Exploring Nature with a Map and Compass*. Farsta: SISU Sport Books.
McNeill, Carol, Cory-Wright, Jean and Renfrew, Tom (1998). *Teaching Orienteering (2nd Edition)*. Duone: Harveys, and Champaign: Human Kinetics.